GOTTA LOOK UP!

Unplug, Reconnect, and Rediscover Life

TOM CAMPBELL

GOTTA LOOK UP!
Unplug, Reconnect, and Rediscover Life
Copyright © 2025 by Tom Campbell

This book is a work of nonfiction based on the author's personal memories, interpretations, and experiences. While every effort has been made to ensure accuracy, certain details, events, and conversations may have been reconstructed or adapted for narrative purposes.

The publisher and author disclaim any liability or responsibility for any actions taken or not taken based on the information in this book. The views expressed herein are solely those of the author and do not necessarily reflect the views or opinions of the publisher or any affiliated parties.

No portion of this book may be reproduced, stored in a retrieval system, or transmitted in any form or by any means—electronic, mechanical, photocopy, recording, scanning, or other—except for brief quotations in critical reviews or articles, without the prior written permission of the publisher.

Requests for information should be addressed to:
info@bluehatpublishing.com

Blue Hat
PUBLISHING

Softcover ISBN: 978-1-962674-42-3
eBook ISBN: 978-1-962674-43-0

Cover design: Rachael Mitchell
Interior design: Jessica Arnett

Printed in China

CONTENTS

PART III: LOOK AHEAD! WHAT KIND OF LIFE DO YOU WANT?

PART IV: LOOK HIGHER AND DEEPER

PART V: KEEP GOING...WE'LL GET THERE!

To my father and mother.
It is an honor to be your son.

To Grant and Ashley.
Being your father is the greatest
honor I will ever have.

Terri:

Keep Looking Up!
Enjoy the next chapter in
your journey!

Tom Clayhill

INTRODUCTION

"If there's a book that you want to read,
but it hasn't been written yet,
then you must write it."

— Toni Morrison

"Call me Ishmael" would have been a great way to start this book, but Herman Melville already took that line to start his masterpiece, Moby Dick. Moby Dick is probably my favorite book of all time so a shout out to Mr. Melville in my first book seems appropriate.

So...call me Tom! I am writing this book because, as Toni Morrison suggests, I believe it must be written. All 8 billion of us on this planet are writing a story that is uniquely ours. All of us experience highs and lows, sadness and joy, ups and downs. I am writing this book to share some of my experiences, hoping that at least one reader will be inspired by some of my successes or learn from some of my mistakes to change their life in a positive way. Hopefully, it will be more than one person!

My initial purpose with *Gotta Look Up* was to help parents get their kids off their smartphones and video games to spend more time interacting face to face with other people. As I journeyed down this path, my *Gotta Look Up* mission expanded from just looking up from our devices to engaging with the world around us, finding new causes and purposes, helping others by sharing our stories, and leaving a trail so that those facing similar challenges can learn from our collective experiences.

For me personally, this *Gotta Look Up* journey was even more profound and rewarding. I was asked and led to look up even higher, to deepen and grow my faith, and to develop a stronger relationship with my God.

The *Gotta Look Up* mission has evolved and is based on five pillars:

1. **Gotta Look Up:** Lift your head up proud. Look up from your screens. See what you're missing.

2. **Gotta Look Around:** Find opportunities to engage in joyful activities, connect with your fellow humans and nature.

3. **Gotta Look Ahead:** What does the future hold? How can you prepare for it through education, financial planning, personal health, and evolving with purpose?

4. **Gotta Look Higher and Deeper:** Improve your spiritual relationships with your Creator, yourself, nature, and the universe.

5. **Gotta Keep Going:** We were all put on this Earth with unique gifts and unique purpose(s) in a pre-determined timeframe. We must keep going no matter what we face. We cannot quit! The only way out is through. We all end up in the same place. We need to love and help each other on that journey.

In addition to these five pillars, the *Gotta Look Up* movement is also based on the belief that there is a lot we can learn during our journey here on earth from each other as people, countries, and from our collective global history. As a result of my passion for learning new things, you will find quotes in each chapter from various sources that have impacted me on this journey, and I hope they will have an impact on you as well.

Collecting these quotes also inspired some thoughts of my own. I call these creations of mine "Tom-isms ," and I have sprinkled them throughout the book. I hope you find them interesting, if not compelling. For your first **TOM-ISM:**

"Your front door is a better portal to the world than your smartphone."

The great French author, Emile Zola, once said:

"We are like books. Most people only see our cover, the minority read only the introduction, many people believe the critics. Few will know our content."

I hope you read past this introduction, and I hope that the contents of this book bring you some entertainment, inspiration, joy, knowledge, and a new perspective on life!

LET'S GO! GOTTA LOOK UP!

PART I

LOOK UP! SEE WHAT YOU'RE MISSING

CHAPTER 1

KEEP YOUR HEAD UP!

"So long as the memory of certain beloved
friends lives in my heart, I shall
say that life is good."

—Helen Keller

"Go outside, to the fields, enjoy nature and the
sunshine, go out and try to recapture happiness in
yourself, think of all the beauty that's still left
in and around you and be happy."

—Anne Frank

You can't go anywhere today without seeing people staring at a screen, thumbing away and missing the world around them. We've all seen it. People walking down the street, heads down, eyes on their phones, oblivious to the world around them.

I was walking down the street years ago when I was rudely bumped into by someone. This person was so engaged with his device that he was not looking where he was going nor paying attention to the people or the world around him. After he bumped into me, he said nothing and continued his zombie walk down the street. I stopped, turned, and said, "Hey, you gotta' look up!" And in that moment, *Gotta Look Up* was born.

Our world is changing faster and faster, and the double-edged sword of technology is changing how we live, how we engage each other, and how we interact with the world. Some of these changes are very positive. Some of them are detrimental if not outright dangerous.

These ubiquitous screens, devices , and applications are distracting and distancing us from our instincts as an animal species, and are therefore distancing us from each other, our children, our friends and families, and our God.

We see people out to eat, looking down at their devices and at the keyboard not talking to the people around them, and maybe even texting them instead. We've even been these people ourselves, not present or engaging with the other people around the table! We play video games for hours or even live in an "alt meta-verse" wearing a virtual reality headset, not in the real world. We text each other while sitting at the same table or in the same house. And most dangerous to our health, we text and fiddle with our smartphones while driving down the freeway at maximum speed or through busy city streets.

Human interaction is becoming digitized. Limited human touch and interaction is not good for us as a species or a society. We need to pay more attention to the world around us. We are focused on looking down, not looking up.

We need to change our trajectory and encourage people to be conscious of their devices and screen time to improve their lives by engaging the world around them. We need to get back to face-to-face conversations, human connection, and pursuing life goals and dreams through action, activities, and learning. We need to strike a balance between real life and technology.

The best portal to the outside world is your front door, not your smartphone or some other screen. Screens aren't a substitute for real relationships just as the photos they take never quite capture the exact colors of a spectacular sunset, a rainbow, an animal in nature, or a field of flowers.

My kids are among the first generation to grow up with smartphones, video games, and other screens as a pervasive part of the culture. I feel as though I failed my children by not balancing their time on these devices with other activities like riding bikes, hiking, playing sports, taking music lessons, or just playing outside and using their imaginations. We don't have to look far to see the downside of what we've enabled.

According to the U.S. Centers for Disease Control, suicide rates for young people have grown dramatically since 2007, around the same time smartphones became more ubiquitous. This could be coincidence, causation, or something in the middle. Either way, we must face this problem as a society and do more to protect our young people from getting caught in the quicksand of devices.

Don't let technology get in the way of living your life. Try to adopt a habit of "positive screen time." Use your screen time for productivity, or for learning something new that you can apply to your life. And yes, use it for entertainment. Just don't get lost in scrolling hour after hour while your most precious resource, time, ticks away.

Instead of clicking a "like," reach out to someone and tell them what you like and why you like it! Instead of watching your son or daughter's game or event through your phone while recording it, watch it live. Make eye contact with them. Focus on their face and emotions in the present.

My hope is that people will recognize that the real world is better than the virtual worlds that technology creates. I hope that I can help people achieve a work, life, *and* technology balance. We are so connected now that we have more "communications" and less conversations. The smartphone is the new looking glass that we all have gone through into a perceived wonderland. The portal to instant gratification that peaks our dopamine may be making us all dopier.

I believe there is a better way. A way that leverages technology as a tool for human improvement rather than a compass that points us everywhere, yet nowhere in particular. I believe that if we are more conscious of our screen time, we will leverage it properly for productivity and get back to real humanity, connection, and nature through our eyes rather than the small lenses of our smartphone cameras.

I truly believe that a better life is lived by harnessing the power of your technology, but only if YOU are the master of IT. Devices are powerful conveniences that can help us be more educated and more efficient if used properly. It's a double-edged sword as these same devices can be addictive time sinks that drain our energy along with its battery.

LOOK UP! See what you're missing!

LOOK AROUND! There's a whole world out there!

LOOK AHEAD! How can you be more aware of your screen time and make it more productive?

CHAPTER 2

GET YOU AND YOUR KIDS OFF THE SCREENS!

"All children need a laptop. Not a computer, but a human laptop. Moms, Dads, Grannies and Grandpas, Aunts, Uncles – someone to hold them, read to them, teach them. Loved ones who will embrace them and pass on the experience, rituals and knowledge of a hundred previous generations. Loved ones who will pass to the next generation their expectations of them, their hopes, and their dreams."

— Colin Powell

"We do well to unplug regularly. Quiet time restores focus and composure."

— Daniel Goleman

I believe every parent has experienced the challenge, and occasional frustration, of keeping their kids away from new technologies that previous generations did not quite understand. When I was a young boy, I remember my mom and dad telling us not to watch so much TV and not to sit too close to the screen.

After school, my brothers and I would finish our homework, grab our baseball gloves, and walk down to the corner of the street to sit on the curb and wait for dad to come home from work. My dad loved baseball and was always up to play catch with his kids. We would sit and wait to see the silver blue nose of our 1964 Rambler make a right turn towards us. The minute he rounded the corner, we would jump up and cheer. Dad would pull into the garage, run in the house, change out of his suit, grab his glove, and come out to play catch with us.

So, how do we engage our kids with similar experiences in an age where the distractions of the world are mere clicks away? I think it starts, as I guess it always has, by identifying areas of interest and finding fulfilling activities for our kids that they will find more engaging than their devices. In a child's early years, I believe this is easier, even though there are screens targeted at babies and toddlers. Some activities you can do with smaller children are taking them for a walk, taking them to the park, and playing with them in the backyard. Younger children love being outside to explore. When they are little, we are their world, so it is easier to control their environment and their experiences. That said, it is still tempting to use those toys and videos, whether you're at home or in the car, to keep them distracted and entertained on trips, or while working, or getting things done around the house. I would be aware of this habit and try to reduce the amount of time they spend watching screens.

So, how do we do our best to help our children manage these new and very powerful technologies as tools and not let them become time sinks? We need to lead by example. I believe it gets more and more difficult the older our kids get, as peer pressure and group inclusion enter the social equation. Remember, your kids are always watching and learning from you.

There are times when conversation via text message or work via email or video call are necessary. Sometimes the timing doesn't perfectly coordinate with the role of parent or caregiver. It takes wise judgment to regulate and balance the necessity of important tasks with the value of spending time with family, children or grandchildren. If you are engaged in a conversation or text exchange on your phone and your child comes up to you, let them know that you need to finish whatever business you are engaged in and then they will have your full attention. Use your best judgement on how to regulate this. You can pause your business, quickly address your child's issue, then get back to or, you can quickly finish your business and then devote your full time and presence to your child.

However, during the time you've purposefully set aside to be with your kids, put the phone away and give them your attention, even if they are playing in the park and you are sitting on a park bench. The phone can wait!

How do you balance the need for kids to learn and manage technology for their future while keeping them from sinking into the quicksand of apps and algorithms?

1. Start them young. Control access to their devices. Don't just leave them lying around the house. Put them up somewhere where they are not seen, so your kids need to ask you for them.

2. Regardless of age, set a daily screen time budget. This includes a screen time budget for you as well!

3. Let them earn more screen time by:
   → Doing chores around the house
   → Getting good grades
   → Displaying good behavior, or going above and beyond on their own accord

4. Challenge them to put their phones, computers, and TVs away for an hour and replace that time with:
   → Bike riding
   → Playing board games
   → Playing sports
   → Reading
   → Spending time in nature
   → Playing music
   → Other activities and hobbies

Engage in these activities listed in Item #4 above with your children to build bonds, experiences, and memories!

5. Lead by example!
    → Don't use your phone in the car!
    → Don't use your phone at the dinner table!
    → Be present when your children approach you with a question or a request. Put the phone down and engage with them.
    → Be present when someone is conversing with you in public. Put the phone away and have a human interaction.
    → Tell your kids that you are reducing your screen time in favor of personal health and wellness. You can prioritize:
      • Reading
      • Exercising
      • Silence, meditation, prayer
      • Calling or meeting with a friend
      • Taking a walk
      • Riding a bike
      • Playing with your pets

The key is making the effort and then being consistent. Set up a daily or weekly "device-free" time and stick to it, much like you would set up a regular "date night" with your spouse or significant other. Turn off all notifications on the device so that you are not distracted by any buzzing, sounds, or beeping!

If you are going to use screens, watch a movie or TV show together! But all other devices need to go into a bowl where they cannot be used during the movie or TV show. And again, all notifications are turned off, or better yet, the device itself is shut off.

Managing screen time, either for ourselves or our children, is an evolution not a revolution. It's hard to change behavior, especially if it's an addictive one. Like any change, it might feel uncomfortable to be without your phone here and there, but over time, you will start managing that device instead of it managing you.

TECHNOFERENCE

Do your best not to engage in "technoference." According to Merriam-Webster "technoference refers to the interruptions in interpersonal communication caused by attention paid to personal technological devices." Technoference occurs when we shift our focus away from our children, our work, or our friends in favor of our devices. When it's easier to pay attention to a smartphone instead of your child's athletic event or music recital, you are suffering from technoference. We have all missed special moments because we were texting. So many of us watch our child's events through our phones instead of with our eyes. These are examples of technoference.

We are guilty of technoference when our kids say:

1. "Why are you always on your phone?"

2. "Look at me!"

3. "You're not listening to me!"

When our kids say these things, we should examine how often we are on our phones around our kids. We should put them away to be present with our children. Our kids are watching and learning, so put the phone away when you are with them, especially if you're attending one of their important events. Take the phone out for a picture or video, but don't miss out on experiencing the performance with your own eyes.

One of my favorite people, from a church men's group I attended while my kids were young, was a gentleman named Art.

Art had already raised his kids, and he was an empty nester. He told us younger dads a story and gave us advice for not missing "home run moments." Art's son had a baseball game one evening, and Art stayed a little late at work to finish some things up. He arrived at the game to find a lot of celebration and cheering. Art's son had hit a home run, and he missed it! He missed it because he worked late. His advice to us was to get to the game on time and never miss a "home run moment." In Art's case, he was not at the game, but it's easy to miss "home run moments" while at an event if we're paying more attention to our phones than the event itself

I will always cherish the time my dad spent with my brothers and me after work playing catch. His presence and time spent face to face made a lasting impression on all of us. After my dad passed away many years later, my brother made us each a keychain with a lace of leather from dad's favorite baseball mitt. I always carry it with me. It not only reminds me of my dad, but more importantly, it reminds me of the valuable time he spent with me. It reminds me to do the same with the people around me.

LOOK UP! See what you're missing! Get yourself and your kids off the screens! Put the phone away, and focus on time with your kids!

LOOK AROUND! Find things that you can do in your community with your children one-on-one or as a family that get them either using their brains or moving around!

LOOK AHEAD! A life with less screen time is a happier existence in the long run!

BIRTHDAYS AND HOLIDAYS

"Christmas is doing a little something
extra for someone."

—Charles M. Schulz

"I am grateful for what I am and have. My
thanksgiving is perpetual."

—Henry David Thoreau

"Every day is a new opportunity to begin again.
Every day is your birthday."

—Dalai Lama

When I was a young boy, holidays were always exciting and something to look forward to, mostly because they involved time with family and friends, good food, games, and sometimes presents! I also enjoyed what were secondary holidays, or days that held some sort of significance, like April Fool's Day or Flag Day. Now, there are so many "International Days of 'blank,'" the holidays that used to be so special now have more competition. And while I can appreciate International Elephant Day or International Cheeseburger Day, my family and friends are not getting together for those to make lifelong memories.

As a Christian, my main religious holidays are Christmas and Easter. In my country, the main holidays are Martin Luther King Day, Presidents Day, Memorial Day, Independence Day, Labor

Day, Veteran's Day, and Thanksgiving. While not official holidays, St. Patrick's Day, April Fool's Day, and Halloween also bring fun to our lives, with Halloween being the most popular of these. The bottom line is that all these dates are set aside because they represent something important to be observed or remembered. It is important to develop traditions for each of these holidays and pass them along to future generations. While many of these days have indeed been derived from actual "holy days" in the Christian calendar, they have been secularized to a large degree. This is not a bad thing in my opinion because it allows those outside of a religion to learn more about their cultural importance, build community with their neighbors, and participate in the fun. It is also interesting to learn about what other cultures celebrate for holidays such as Hannukah, Diwali, Eid, and others.

BIRTHDAYS

Although not holidays, it is important to commemorate and celebrate birthdays, whether they be our own or those of the people who are most important in our lives. If someone is important to you, it is important to remember them on their special day. Most people these days will be reminded of someone's birthday via social media and send them a quick message. This is the bare minimum! Better to send them a handwritten card, give them a call to wish them a happy birthday, or best yet, celebrate with them in person.

Birthdays are special to me because my parents made them so, especially my mom. My mom would always ask us what kind of meal and what flavor of cake and ice cream we wanted. She always made us a home-cooked birthday dinner and baked a cake. My go-to was vanilla cake with brown sugar frosting. My dinner request varied. "Store bought" was not in my mom's vocabulary when it came to birthdays.

THANKSGIVING

Thanksgiving has always been one of my favorite holidays. The short week at school or work that came with it. The great food and my mom's cooking. The lead-up to Christmas.

The National Day of Thanks was established on the fourth Thursday in November by Abraham Lincoln. As a result, we get a four-day weekend, a great turkey dinner, parades, and pro football on television throughout the day. I highly recommend you add another ritual to the day: a Thanksgiving football game.

Our Thanksgiving Day football game first started with a bunch of high school friends getting together to play touch football, rain or shine. One time, it did rain...hard! And it was a memorable mess. As we got older and started our own families, it became more of a family event than a friend event. And as family moved further away, I continued to host the annual game with a combination of family members that lived nearby, high school friends in the area, and I extended the tradition to new friends and families of my children's classmates.

Here's how you set up a Thanksgiving Football Game.

1. Buy a football and some orange cones to mark the field.

2. I highly recommend investing in a pair of football shoes as well.

3. Order bagels, donuts, and coffee ahead of time, and put them on a folding table.

4. Get a cooler full of ice, and fill it with water, juice, and some cream cheese and jelly for the bagels.

5. Make your own trophy to award to the MVP (We called it the "Most Visible Player" rather than the "Most

Valuable Player" because the award had more to do with who made the game the most fun vs. who had the best performance.)

6. Get packs of football cards and See's Candies Lollipops to give to the kids afterwards. Buy extras because the adults will want them too!

7. Put out a container as a donation box for charity. Ask people, especially the kids, to bring their loose change to fill up the donation box. Make sure to let them know what good cause they are supporting.

8. At halftime, you can add a turkey bowling game while everyone is getting refreshments. Get a frozen turkey and some plastic bowling pins. Line them up and let everyone take a turn heaving the turkey at the pins. This feature was added by my friend Steve Foster one year and was a big hit.

THE CAMPBELL CUP

I mentioned earlier that when you plan a game, you should make a trophy.

The original Campbell Cup has been lost to the ages. It consisted of a piece of railroad tie with a small trophy at the top and two handles on the side. It was created and built by my dad.

The trophy was given to the most outstanding player, but that didn't mean it was based on the best performance. Outstanding meant that they did something remarkable during the event. One year, my mom won it in a family football game because she lost her balance and ended up recovering a fumble by sitting on it!

The rule was that if you won the Campbell Cup, you had three obligations:

1. You must display it in a prominent, non-garage or basement, room in the house until the next event.

2. You were required to add something to the trophy prior to the next event.

3. You were involved in choosing who it was awarded to at the next event.

The second version of the Campbell Cup was started by my brother, Jim. He took a surplus silver vase from his wedding gifts, and this became the start of the new Campbell Cup. Since I won it that year, I added a wooden base and a Campbell's Soup can. As part of the wooden base, I started a name list so that each winner could write his or her name and the year they won in Sharpie on the trophy. It wasn't the same as the Stanley Cup, but it had the same spirit. Unfortunately, the second Campbell Cup is also gone. Maybe someday I'll make a new one for my grandkids.

Thanksgiving Football is one of my treasured memories. Even though it is now just a memory, I get messages every year from people mentioning how much fun it was and how their kids continue to talk about it. Some have even started their own games. It would be fun to see if they have built their own trophies as well!

CHRISTMAS

I love Christmas! Who wouldn't? Suddenly, there is a tree inside of the house with lights and ornaments on it. Houses in the neighborhood are decorated with lights and ornaments as well. Some would argue that the secular part of Christmas doesn't matter, that Jesus is the "reason for the season." Yes, He is, but

I think the Jesus I know would be happy that His birthday is celebrated by making children smile, bringing families together, singing carols, sharing good food, and exchanging gifts.

While gifts seem to be the central point of Christmas, what I remember most is the magic that my parents made during the Christmas season. I tried to pass down that same magic to my children. The excitement of giving and receiving is what touched me the most, and it still does. Christmas is magic, and that magic should be preserved, whether you choose to go fully religious or fully secular in your approach. Jesus is the reason for the season, but so were mom and dad. Jesus was always a big part of our Christmas celebration. The nativity scene had a prominent place on the mantle over the fireplace in the main room of our house, right across from the Christmas tree. I firmly believe that Jesus knows he doesn't have to compete with Santa Claus. Santa Claus is just a vehicle to remind us to give and to create magic in honor of His birthday. I believe that Jesus is pleased when we give to one another out of love and when we are the source of happiness to others in His name, regardless of the date.

LOOK UP! What are the holidays that are most important to you and your family?

LOOK AROUND! Who might be alone on their birthday or other important holidays this year unless you reach out to them?

LOOK AHEAD! How do you want to celebrate your birthday? Who do you want to celebrate it with?

KEEP GOING! Learn something about other cultures and their holidays. If you have friends who celebrate, they will be happy to share the details and might even invite you to participate!

CHAPTER 4

CONCENTRIC CIRCLES OF RELATIONSHIPS

"Crocodiles are easy. They try to kill and eat you.
People are harder. Sometimes they
pretend to be your friend first."

—Steve Irwin

"A journey is best measured in friends,
rather than miles."

—Tim Cahill

Recently, I was pondering the breadth and depth of certain relationships in my life. I tried to understand why there seem to be certain people who are always available and there for me, while others seem to be happy with a "drive-by relationship."

We all have those relationships with people who we see occasionally and would like to spend more time with, but they just never seem to be available...unless they need or want something from you.

On the other side of the spectrum are our "ride or die" or "BFF" relationships. This is usually a very small handful of close and trusted friends.

We also have those people in our lives that are very important, but live a distance away, so we don't get to interact with them as much. But the minute we are back together, it's like time never passed because there is such a shared bond, comfort level, and trust that we pick up right where we left off.

A concentric circle is two or more circles with a common center. Each concentric circle will have a different radius but the same center point, which is also called a mid-point. Think of a slow-motion video of a water ripple, generated after a single drop impacts a calm surface. From the center of impact, waves radiate outward, ever growing, ever expanding, but the point of impact, the center, remains. This represents you.

In looking at this concept of social circles, I began to think more in depth about my personal relationships and how to define the concentric circles, or spheres of relationships, that we all have in our lives. The first and most important relationship you need to invest in is the one with yourself. The concentric circles of self are your soul, your heart, your mind, and your body. How we take care of these core components is the priority. We cannot have concentric circles of relationships without first establishing and strengthening the center of every relationship, which is ourselves!

I have long believed that we go about our lives forming concentric circles of relationships. We establish circles of relationships based on their importance and closeness to us over the course of our lives. We then invest our limited time and resources appropriately to preserve the relationship, grow it, or let it go. Based on life stage and circumstances, we either move people closer to the center circle or to the outer edges of our relationship universe.

After some consideration, I created the following list of relationship circles. I may decide to add more as time passes, but for now I think this is a pretty good place to start:

Center Point:	You! Your Soul - Your Heart, Mind, and Physical being
Circle One:	Inner Circle: Family - Children - Best friends
Circle Two:	Circle of Trust: Extended family - Close Friends That Are Like Family
Circle Three:	Familiar Acquaintances: Co-workers - Business partners - Neighbors – Spiritual Leaders
Circle Four:	Random Acquaintances: People we've met and may continue to see or meet.- The barista - The bank teller - The store clerk
Circle Five:	People We Have Let Go Of but Let Back In: People who were once an important part of our lives, but we've lost touch. Facebook Friends - LinkedIn Business Connections
Circle Six:	Targeted Strangers: People we don't know yet but would like to meet. Mentors - Crushes who we haven't approached yet - Hiring Managers
Circle Seven:	Strangers: People we don't know yet but may meet sometime in the future.
Circle Eight:	The Unwelcomed: People we've met but don't ever want to interact with again - People we never want to meet.

We tend to move people in and out of these spheres based on both an individual and mutual willingness to invest in the relationship. For example, new acquaintances can move from Random Acquaintance to Close Friend to Inner Circle over time if the concentric circles match up and the relationship evolves in a mutually beneficial and positive way. The beauty of our lives is that we get to determine who gets close to us and where they fit in the concentric circles or spheres of our life. While some may try to improve their position in our concentric sphere, we ultimately determine where they belong in our lives and what importance to give that relationship.

Also, we cannot choose where we fit into anyone else's concentric circles of relationships. While we may want to have a closer relationship with someone we love, they have a say based on their life stage or situation, what is important to them, and where they prioritize their life and time investments. This shouldn't be taken personally or as rejection, but as reality in terms of how people prioritize their lives and what time they are willing to free up to invest in a relationship. Everyone has life priorities and limited time! This doesn't mean we should give up on improving our relationship with someone who is important to us. We can still invite them to a closer circle, but we shouldn't do so with any specific expectation or do so in a way that is obsessive and unhealthy for both parties.

So, think for a minute about your relationships. How do you define your concentric circles? Who falls into what sphere? Is anyone in a specific circle that you would like to invite into a closer one? Is there someone in a closer circle that should be let go? It is an interesting way to look at things and can bring clarity to your life in terms of where you prioritize and invest your limited, precious resource of time.

Reach out to some friends that you haven't engaged with in some time to plan for coffee, a meal, or just to get together to have some fun. We've "Gotta Look Up" from our devices and into the faces of the people with whom we want to have better relationships.

"Of all the means which wisdom acquires to ensure happiness throughout the whole of life, by far the most important is friendship."

— Epicurus

"Friends are God's way of taking care of us."

— Unknown

TOM-ISM: "It's better to SHARE your life with someone, than to SPEND your life with someone."

LOOK UP! Who falls in which concentric circle in your current life? Who's important to you who you haven't spoken to in a while?

LOOK AROUND! Who would you like to bring closer to you? Who would you like to move away from?

LOOK AHEAD! Get out there, and start working on expanding your concentric circles!

CHAPTER 5

HAPPINESS

"Happiness is like a butterfly. The more you chase it,
the more it will elude you,
But if you turn your attention to other things,
It will come and sit softly on your shoulder."

—Henry David Thoreau

"Live and be happy, and make others so."

—Mary Shelley

We all strive for it. We all want it for ourselves, our family, and our friends. Happiness is one of the deepest desires in life along with love, companionship, purpose, and health.

But happiness is elusive. Mostly because people look for it in the material, the superficial, and the irrelevant. Some people look for it on social media or by living vicariously through entertainers or professional athletes.

I would propose that happiness originates from within each of us and can be expanded by our external experiences and interactions.

Happiness is easier to find when:

- → You find it within you.
- → You find it in the simple things.
- → You find it in experiences rather than material things.

→ You have people around you who are interested in maximizing it with you.

→ You find a little bit of it every day!

How does one measure happiness? There is no 2 + 2 = 4 equation because happiness is not linear, it is geometric and multidimensional. Each of us will define happiness in our own unique way, tied to our life interests, purposes, and goals. You can choose to be happy, but it requires an open heart, open mind, and discipline to focus on the specific things that are important. Do not get lost in the noise of how society defines happiness or in comparing your situation to others in a way that creates envy or jealousy.

I am happier when I focus on the blessings in life rather than what is missing from my life. I experience more joy when I enhance my skill set and learn new things, when I experience new places, and when I set and achieve realistic goals. I wasn't happy when I was focused on getting more, comparing my life to someone else, striving toward a better job title that paid more, wanting a "better" car, which usually meant a more expensive one, or eating out too often rather than cooking at home. All of these choices were tied to what other people were doing and not to what was the best decision for me or my family.

HAPPINESS AND THE CONCEPT OF ENOUGH

We've all had days that test us and the depth of our faith. We've all had our unique trials and tribulations. When these days happen, happiness seems distant. I had one such day when all seemed lost, and it caused me to re-evaluate my life, re-examine what was most important, and set a new course.

During the night of that particular day, I did not sleep. I prayed. I talked to God. I apologized to Him for getting lost in comparison, envy, greed, and the pursuit of more. I asked for His help in repairing my life. I asked Him for "just enough." Enough to take care of myself, my son, and my daughter, to give them a comfortable life, and to help them pursue their passions and careers. I also promised Him that whatever excess there was above "enough," I would put to good use to help others, donate to charities, or save up for my family's future.

The concept of "enough" will change as your life evolves and your needs change. "Enough" will be defined differently by each person in different stages of their life. But the power in the concept of "enough" is that it drives us toward satisfaction instead of greed. "Enough" is still an abundance mindset because it is not a cap or ceiling, it is a floor. It is the basics of what you need to live a comfortable life. Anything you achieve above your "enough" can be shared with others or invested for a rainy day when you might need a little more to have enough. You get to define what "enough" means to you. You get to ask for "enough."

The teachings of Buddha offer us the following proverb to consider:

"Enough is a feast."

And the stoic, Seneca, offers the following:

"You ask what is the proper limit to a person's wealth? First, having what is essential, and second, having what is enough."

And Mahatma Gandhi offers the following around the concept of "enough:"

"Earth provides enough to satisfy every man's need, but not every man's greed."

So, is your "enough" tied to the necessities needed to live a comfortable and simple life, or is it tied to the pursuit of more and more?

There's a well-known prayer that contains the line, "Give us this day, our daily bread." That line is the greatest endorsement ever for the concept of "enough."

TOM-ISM: "Your overall happiness is based on your personal definition and execution of the 'Concept of Enough.'"

THE QUADRATIC FORMULA FOR HAPPINESS

Here's some good news for you! Remember algebra? Well, you get to use it again! Sort of! To those who say that you own your happiness, I wholeheartedly agree, but I would contend that there are many external variables that have an impact on your happiness. Thus, my theory of "The Quadratic Formula for Happiness."

If you remember your middle school or high school algebra classes, it looks like this:

$$x = \frac{-b \pm \sqrt{b^2 - 4ac}}{2a}$$

The purpose of the quadratic formula was to solve…(Insert record scratch noise in your mind here!)

Actually, who cares? I never really used that formula outside of those math classes. But I did tell you that we would use algebra to calculate our happiness variables and happiness equation.

Here are the variables that I would propose for my Quadratic Formula For Happiness theory... and conveniently, they spell ALGEBRA:

A = Awareness (of what makes you happy)

L = Love

G = Grace (or you can substitute "Gratitude" or "Growth")

E = Empathy

B = Buddies (friends and family), or you can substitute with "Boundaries"

R = Resilience (Keep Going), or Reasons (Purpose)

A = Alignment (with your Purpose)

We are all the owners of our own happiness. But that is too simple an answer for such a complex and important concept. There are external factors and variables like people, jobs, relationships, health, finances, etc. that can:

- → Add to our happiness!
- → Subtract from it.
- → Multiply our happiness!
- → Divide it.
- → Make our happiness exponential!

Who or what make up your happiness variables? Maximize the time you spend with those people, in those places, and with those things. And if you want a simpler formula, you can look to Paulo Coelho's quote that "Happiness is multiplied when it is divided."

COMPARISON AND HAPPINESS

There is a saying that "comparison is the thief of joy." I like this statement a lot, as it pertains to the social media phenomenon of "FOMO" or "Fear of Missing Out." We see people having the time of their lives on various social media apps and think that this one snapshot of a moment in time defines their entire day or life. It doesn't! I live in Los Angeles and have seen my share of people taking posed or staged photographs in an attempt to get the perfect shot for "The Gram." I've seen lines form so that each person can take their turn posing in front of a sign, a restaurant, a star on the sidewalk, or a plate of food. If we compare our daily lives to someone else's based on their social media feeds, we need to go back and study our ALGEBRA!

Comparison can be a thief of joy, but if properly harnessed, comparison can also give us "belief in joy," especially when it reinforces how good we actually have it. We can use comparison not as a path to envy, but to understand what skills, characteristics, or strategies have been employed by others that we need to learn, develop, and implement to reach our desired goals and aspirations.

I continue to like the phrase, "There but for the grace of God go I." This is also where comparison can give us belief in joy. I have suffered through a divorce, but others have suffered through loss of a relationship due to death of a loved one or child. While I do not delight in the fact that their outcome is worse than mine, the ability to compare my situation with someone who is living through greater difficulty makes me both thankful and empathetic to those going through a worse hell than mine.

When you focus on the concept of "enough" and define your happiness variables, you will likely find that comparison is minimized because you will be operating from a position where you better understand what makes you happy. This will minimize your need for comparison.

Our individual happiness is up to each of us. Let's remember what the painter, Bob Ross once said: "It's so important to do something every day that will make you happy."

"Happiness is a choice, not a result. Nothing will make you happy until you choose to be happy. No person will make you happy unless you decide to be happy. Your happiness will not come to you. It can only come from you."

— Ralph Marston

"I think the saddest people always try their hardest to make other people happy, because they know what it's like to feel absolutely worthless, and they don't want anyone else to feel like that."

— Robin Williams

"Judge nothing, you will be happy.
Forgive everything, you will be happier.
Love everything, you will be happiest."

— Buddha

TOM-ISM: "Remember, the founding document says, 'Life, Liberty, and the Pursuit of Happiness,' not 'Life, Liberty, and the Pursuit of MORE.'"

LOOK UP! Where do you need to make improvements in your life to pursue your happiness?

LOOK AROUND! Compare, but don't envy. Learn the variables that make up your happiness equation. Make a plan for what you need to do to achieve your happiness.

LOOK AHEAD! Visualize yourself achieving as much happiness as possible! Find happiness each day!

KEEP GOING! "Enough" can be enough.

CHAPTER 6

CONFIDENCE

"We must have perseverance and, above all, confidence in ourselves. We must believe that we are gifted for something, and that this thing, at whatever cost, must be attained."

—Marie Curie

"You gain strength, courage, and confidence by every experience in which you really stop to look fear in the face. You are able to say to yourself, 'I have lived through this horror. I can take the next thing that comes along.'"

—Eleanor Roosevelt

If I have any regret in life, it is that I did not focus on building my confidence at an early age. Confidence is built through taking action. It is built through trial and error and by overcoming those errors to achieve success, or at least to be better than you were the day before. I have experienced people telling me that I wasn't good enough, that I didn't have the talent to achieve certain goals, and that I didn't have the skills. These were terrible things for anyone to say to a kid, but it was more terrible that I believed them. I wasted time and energy seeking revenge and proving them wrong rather than just ignoring their opinions and moving forward to what was most important to me. Knowing the importance of self-confidence and resilience is to lead a successful life. I do my best to teach my children and other young people to believe in their capabilities and to seek help from experts to learn new skills. Even experts had to start from zero and build confidence in their abilities along the way. Taking action, learning, practicing, and developing good habits leads to increased knowledge, skills, and confidence.

Confidence = Courage + Action + Learning + Adjusting

Confidence is different from courage. Courage is facing a danger or risk. You can be courageous without confidence, or you can be courageous with confidence.

Confidence is different from faith. Faith is belief in something unseen. Confidence is the knowledge and attitude that you have properly prepared for something or that you have a natural skill set that will win the day.

Confidence is self-belief. Confidence is trust in your abilities and skills. Confidence is knowing that whatever comes your way, you will overcome. Maybe not right now. Maybe not today. Maybe not tomorrow, but sometime in the future, you will overcome the obstacles put in front of you.

Confidence is also built through education. According to Confucius, "Education breeds confidence. Confidence breeds hope. Hope breeds peace." The next step in building confidence is to put your newfound education into practice, and take new action with new skills. The great Dale Carnegie said, "Inaction breeds doubt and fear. Action breeds confidence and courage." One builds confidence by setting goals, taking action, learning and adjusting, taking further action, and repeating these steps until the target is reached.

LOOK UP! This is the first step to confidence! Keep your head up high!

LOOK AROUND! What do you want to accomplish or learn? Who can help you get there?

LOOK AHEAD! What is your plan for success? What steps do you need to take to get started?

KEEP GOING! Try. Fail. Learn and adjust! Try again! Fail some more! Learn and adjust! Rinse and repeat!

CHAPTER 7

ALIGNMENT AND PURPOSE

"You cannot get through a single day without having an impact on the world around you. What you do makes a difference, and you have to decide what kind of difference you want to make."

— Jane Goodall

"The question isn't who is going to let me, it's who is going to stop me."

— Ayn Rand

Sometimes we ask big questions. "What am I doing here?" "What is in this for me?" "How does this serve my true purpose?" We say things like, "There's got to be more to life than this." Do these sound familiar? How often do you ask these types of questions?

Where do these types of thoughts originate? I think they are triggered when our purpose is out of alignment with our reality. When you are not aligned with your purpose, you get frustrated, depressed, or angry. You have that gut feeling that you are missing out in life. If you get these feelings or hear these voices, listen. Take notes. Start making a plan.

This is why it is important to expose ourselves to different areas of interest. Identify things that "make your heart sing." Passion leads to purpose. That voice you hear in your head or that tug you feel on your soul are nudges toward your purpose. Many people never pursue their passions or their purpose out of fear, doubt, or obligations to family and paying the bills. Now, I'm not saying quit your job today, sell everything you own, and go pursue your passion. What I am saying is, listen to that inner voice. Take a small step toward that purpose. Then take the next small step, and the next, until you are able to transition full-time into your passion pursuit.

Do you have an idea right now about something that you have always wanted to pursue in life but have either never started or never moved forward? This is what I am talking about. I believe that these ideas that pop into our heads are not coincidental. I believe they are planted. They are either planted by divine intervention or were set in motion millions of years ago by a Universe that provides us with the unique talents and abilities to bring these purposes forth. These purposes are tied to our hearts, minds, and souls. They are aligned with the gifts that we are given by our Creator. To not pursue them, even at the slowest of paces, would be a disservice to ourselves, our Creator, to the Universe, and to each other. Pursuing them, even at a basic level, puts us in alignment. It is why we all feel motivated, excited, and fulfilled when we try to apply our gifts and share them with the world.

"YOU SHOULD"

We have many influences over our lives. Parents, teachers, friends, and others. How many times have you heard someone give you advice by starting with the words, "you should?"

You're so smart, you should...be an engineer.

You're so beautiful, you should...be a model.

Parents say this a lot, and it is usually from a place of love. But "you should" can put doubt and barriers on a child. It can typecast them into believing that they should be something not aligned with their heart, their passion, or their purpose. It can also greatly influence a child that does not wish to disappoint their parents.

I will offer this "you should." YOU SHOULD decide what lights a fire in your heart and prioritize pursuing those things and nothing else . Go ahead and seek advice from parents and friends, but ultimately, it's your life and your heart to follow. Go For It!

"Be brave enough to live the life of your dreams according to your vision and purpose instead of the expectations and opinions of others."

— Roy T. Bennett

"Don't be pushed by your problems. Be led by your dreams."

— Ralph Waldo Emerson

Alignment is tied to purpose, and purpose is tied to motivation. What is the source of our motivation? Is it driven by our own souls, by the divine, or by societal, man-made ideas or problems? If we fall into debt, we are motivated to pay it off. If we find someone attractive, we are motivated to get closer to them to learn more about them. If we are lonely, we are motivated to find a friend or a community. If we are hungry or thirsty, we are motivated to find food and water.

"The purpose of life is not to be happy. It is to be useful,
to be honorable, to be compassionate, to have it make some
difference that you have lived and lived well."

— Ralph Waldo Emerson

"Every day, think as you wake up, 'Today, I am
fortunate to be alive, I have a precious human life,
I am not going to waste it."

— The Dalai Lama

"There is no greater gift you can give or receive than
to honor your calling. It's why you were born.
And how you become most truly alive."

— Oprah Winfrey

PURPOSE

Purpose is what drives us. Purpose is part of our core instincts. It is the rudder to our ship. When we are small children, our purpose is to learn. When we become teenagers, our purpose is to continue to learn, to grow, and to look at potential futures. After graduating high school, we continue to discover our talents and apply them to our purpose. We enter a college, find a job, or join a trade that refines our skills and enhances our purpose.

When we have children, our purpose becomes magnified. We are meant to guide the next generation into finding their purpose while we continue to discover and adjust our own. Once this purpose of parenthood is removed, it is easy to feel lost again. To not know what our new purpose should be. Empty nests are opportunities to continue along our original paths of purpose, to add new purposes, or to go in a completely different direction to discover and refine new purposes that we never knew we had.

Your purpose could be big or small, but purpose might be the most important thing driving our lives and our measurement of success. As American evangelist and baseball player Billy Sunday once said, "More men fail through lack of purpose than lack of talent." Many people have talents, but the key is identifying a purpose to align with and using those talents toward a goal or greater good. Talent alone will not be enough.

A purpose-driven life is one of clarity and passion. When you know what your gifts and talents are, and once you have defined your purpose, you will know how to best leverage those gifts to pursue your purpose. This brings satisfaction to your life. You will be living in purpose and moving toward self-actualization.

A person who is distanced from their purpose is a person who is likely lost, depressed, or even angry because they are too far away from their core beliefs and gifts. They are frustrated being stuck in a life that is not in alignment with who they are deep down and what they want to bring to the world and create.

God plants us here at this particular time in history for a specific purpose. It is incumbent upon each of us to pursue that purpose. We are tasked to grow and bear fruit. There is a need in the universe for us to be where we are and do what we do. Fulfill your purpose.

"The purpose of life is not to win. The purpose
of life is to grow and share. When you come to look back
on all that you have done in life, you will get more
satisfaction from the pleasure you brought to other
people's lives than you will from the times that
you outdid and defeated them."

— Harold Kushner

Abraham Maslow was a leading humanistic psychologist, born in Brooklyn, New York in 1908. He developed a philosophical theory around five levels of human needs that we call "Maslow's Hierarchy of Needs." The five levels start with a foundation of "Physiological Need," on top of which we build a layer of "Safety," then "Love and Belonging," then "Esteem," then "Self-Actualization."

Self-Actualization:	Desire to be the most that one can be.
Esteem:	Respect, self-esteem, status, recognition, strength, freedom.
Love and Belonging:	Friendship, intimacy, family, sense of connection.

Safety: Personal security, employment, resources, health, property.

Physiological Need: Air, water, food, shelter, sleep, clothing, reproduction. *

*ThoughtCo

I would argue that "Self-Actualization" is the execution of your purpose, and the alignment of the other hierarchal layers is what paves the way for you to achieve your purpose or to "Self-Actualize." Howard Thurman, author, philosopher, and civil rights activist said it best: "Don't ask yourself what the world needs. Ask yourself what makes you come alive, and go do that, because what the world needs is people who have come alive." "Self-Actualization" is not a monetary goal. It is not a house we buy. It is not what car you drive or what clothing labels you wear. All of these things are biproducts of self-actualization. True "Self-Actualization" is when we come alive to achieve and fulfill our purpose on Earth.

LOOK UP! Get aligned with your purpose! Do you have more than one?

LOOK AROUND! How does your purpose help others and the world? Do you have mentors in your life who can help you get more aligned to your purpose?

LOOK AHEAD! What unfulfilled dreams can you move forward on today?

KEEP GOING! Don't ever give up on fulfilling your purpose!

"Waste no more time talking about what
a good man should be. Be one."

— Marcus Aurelius

"The meaning of life is to find your gift.
The purpose of life is to give it away."

— Pablo Picasso

NOTE TO SELF

"What is my purpose in life?" I asked the void.

"What if I told you that you fulfilled it when you
took an extra hour to talk to that kid
about his life?" said the voice.

"Or when you paid for that young couple in the
restaurant? Or when you saved that dog in traffic?
Or when you tied your father's shoes for him?"

"Your problem is that you equate your purpose with
goal-based achievement. The Universe isn't interested in
your achievements... just your heart. When you choose
to act out of kindness, compassion, and love,
you are already aligned with your true purpose."

"No need to look any further!"

— Author Unknown

CHAPTER 8

FAILURE LEADS TO SUCCESS!

"Not failure, but low aim, is the crime. In great attempts it is glorious even to fail."

—Bruce Lee

"I can accept failure. Everyone fails at something. But I can't accept not trying."

—Michael Jordan

FAILURE

Failure might be the thing in life that we deal with the most. But what exactly is failure? Some define failure as not meeting our desired goals or outcomes. Some say that failures are required stepping stones to success. Real failure is giving in to fear and never starting or giving up on your ideal life vision and goals. But failure is only permanent if one gives up. Once you get started on a path, each failure can be used as a stepping stone to success. It can be a learning process to get one step closer to the right solution. That said, it is important that the goal you're pursuing actually serves you and your gifts. If your goal is to be in the Navy, but you get seasick, then you might want to adjust that goal to joining the Air Force or the Army instead.

I recently heard the phrase "fail forward." When you fail forward, you carry forward momentum with you. You're not stuck, you just need to adjust to move forward again.

"I have not failed. I have found a thousand
ways that won't work."
— Thomas Edison

"Try again. Fail again. Fail better."
— Samuel Beckett

"Failure is simply the opportunity to begin
again more intelligently."
— Henry Ford

"A man is great not because he hasn't failed; a man
is great because failure hasn't stopped him."
— Confucius

SUCCESS

"Ambition is the path to success.
Persistence is the vehicle you arrive in."

—Bill Bradley

"Success isn't about how much money you make. It's
about the difference you make in people's lives."

—Michelle Obama

If you are on social media a lot, it can be difficult to discern who is truly successful and who is faking it. There are a lot of people out there who claim to be "crushing it" who really aren't; they just post a lot on Facebook or Instagram to give the appearance that they are doing well. Many of us develop "FOMO" as a result of looking at what we think are the everyday lives of other people but are truly just highly curated, posed snapshots that are used to convince you of their success. While society tries to define success for us, we actually have a say, and it is important that we know ourselves and our purpose in life well enough that we take that power back and define our own success.

How do you define success? Success should be measured by you and you alone, or maybe with input from the people in your closest inner circle. Ultimately, it's up to you to define. No one can define success for you, as it is deeply personal and aligned with your purpose and your soul.

To find success, you need to take a leap of faith toward your purpose, and discover what is most important to you. Working for someone else for your entire career is one path to success, if that is what makes you happy. Starting your own business is another path to success. But don't let others decide what success means to you. Only you can define it, and you will define it based on your gifts, your skills, and your purpose. Maybe success for you is working just enough to pay your bills and finance a lifestyle that makes you happy, while having more time available to spend on things that interest you. Maybe your definition of success is the big house, the private plane, cars, and wearing fashionable labels. Again, if that makes you happy, then that is success too. Success is entirely up to you!

"To laugh often and much.
To win the respect of smart people
And the affection of children
To earn the approval of honest critics
And face the betrayal of false friends
To appreciate beauty
To find the best in others
To leave the world a bit better
Whether by a healthy child
A garden patch
Or a redeemed social condition
To know one life has breathed easier
Because you have lived
This is to have succeeded."

— Emerson, "To Have Succeeded"

Redefine your meaning of success.
You are successful when you are at peace.
You are successful when you treat
others with compassion.
You are successful when you're living a life that
aligns with your Spirit.
Don't think that success only equates to a high-paying
career and physical wealth.
You are successful when you live a blissful, balanced life filled
with Love, Peace, and growth."

— Meditate and Love

What does success look like to you? I would recommend making a list of what your ideal life would look like. How much time do you want to spend at work? Where do you want to live? Are you going to get married? Do you want to have kids? Do you want to travel the world? Think about all the variables that would make your life successful, and write them down. Then, examine this list, and see where you are in achieving each of these ideal life items. What have you already accomplished? What are you interested in finishing off that is in progress? What haven't you acted on yet, and how can you get started? The tricky part of life is that you are not likely to achieve everything on your list. You may need to change course or change the goal as time passes. Life throws us curveballs, so it is important not to see this as a list of expectations, but look at is as goals. If you have to make adjustments, it doesn't mean that you weren't successful. Booker T. Washington once said about success, "I have learned that success is to be measured not so much by the position that one has reached in life as be the obstacles which he has over-come while trying to succeed." Entrepreneur and author Robert Kiyosaki offers the following: "The size of your success is mea-sured by the strength of your desire, the size of your dream, and how you handle disappointment along the way." We examined failure a little earlier, but given Mr. Kiyosaki's statement, maybe we can redefine "failure" as "disappointment."

There are more ways to measure success than by how much money you make, what type of car you drive, the size of the house you live in, or by your job title. Society's definition of suc-cess does not have to be yours. You get to decide!

"Stop with the idea in your head that one day, when
you are successful, you will 'be somebody.'
You are just as important today as you will be
when you are successful.
Your life matters just as much now as it will later.
Strive to become your best self.
Don't strive to be somebody.
You already are.
You just need to show up in your life.
Be present, and you will have arrived."

— Unknown

"Success is liking yourself,
Liking what you do, and
Liking how you do it."

— Maya Angelou

LOOK UP! How do you define success? How do you define failure?

LOOK AROUND! Make a list of what is most important in your life.

LOOK AHEAD! Visualize the life that you want and take steps toward it!

KEEP GOING! Failure is a temporary disappointment. Learn from your mistakes, re-group, and move forward with new information toward your goals!

CHAPTER 9

FAMILY AND FOUNDATIONS

"Always look for the best in others."

—A.G. Campbell

"Character is how you treat those who can do
nothing for you."

—Unknown

My father was a great man and a tremendous influence on my life. My dad was born on November 11th. As a Navy veteran and patriot, it is fitting that my father was born on Veteran's Day, also known as Armistice Day. This day is commemorated as it marks the end of World War I, the "War to End All Wars."

It is important to study where we came from and what made us who we are as individuals, members of a family, members of a community, and members of a nation. In my case, I go back to thinking about how obviously important my father was, and still is, in my life. He was my second teacher (Mom will always be the first.) He formed the foundation of who I am as a man through what he instilled in me as a child. These teachings were passed down to him by his mother and father and all their mothers and fathers before them.

As a child, there were things I didn't fully understand the meaning, complexity, and nuance of, and I am grateful to understand their importance now. Several messages have stuck with me over the years:

POP'S 10 COMMANDMENTS

My family on my father's side lived on the East Coast, mostly in the Philadelphia area. It is a great city, especially for someone interested in history. In that area of the country, grandparents are commonly called Mom-Mom and Pop-Pop. In our case, my father's father wanted to shorten that moniker and be called "Pop."

I only saw Pop on four occasions. He was a funny man who I wish I had more time with, but his influence was great.

One of the things my dad shared with me was "Pop's 10 Commandments":

Pop's 10 Commandments:

1. Obey God's 10 Commandments

2. Respect Everybody

3. Help Somebody

4. If You Can't Say Good, Don't Say Anything

5. The Youngest First

6. Make Sure Children Are Happy

7. Always Tell The Truth

8. Take Care Of Your Family

9. Thank God For What You Have

10. Always Stick Together

DAD'S TEN COMMANDMENTS
(POP's)

1   OBEY GOD'S TEN COMMANDMENTS

2   RESPECT EVERYBODY

3   HELP SOMEBODY

4   IF YOU CAN'T SAY GOOD, DON'T SAY ANYTHING

5   THE YOUNGEST FIRST

6   MAKE SURE CHILDREN ARE HAPPY

7   ALWAYS TELL THE TRUTH

8   TAKE CARE OF YOUR FAMILY

9   THANK GOD FOR WHAT YOU HAVE

10 ALWAYS STICK TOGETHER

I keep a copy of this list with me in my wallet and look at it whenever I need a quick reset about what is important. I continue to strive to keep all of these, but like God's 10 Commandments, I sometimes fall short. But this list is not a request for perfect behavior, it is a guideline to return to when I come up short.

I SHALL LIVE ON...

Ever since I can remember, there was a plaque on the wall at our house that read as follows:

"Throw My Ashes To The Winds.
Let Not My Name Be Remembered.
For I Shall Live On, My Child, Through You."

I am not sure where this came from. My grandfather may have written it himself. It is a very powerful verse, and it obviously had a long-term impact on me. It shows the pride of father-hood, the importance of lineage and legacy, and the honoring of children. But ultimately, it shows how we can all be immortal by taking care of ourselves, our children, and our grandchildren as they carry our genes, our knowledge, our memories, and our legacy into the future.

A FAMILY LEGACY MATTERS

"Let us so bear ourselves that if our family lives
for a thousand years, men will still say, the
Campbells were honorable people."

— A.G. Campbell

For this one, I do know from where the inspiration came. It is derived from Winston Churchill's "Finest Hour" speech, tout-ing the accomplishments of the vaunted "few," the pilots in the Royal Air Force during the Battle of Britain. It was a victory that changed the course of the world and was Hitler's first defeat in World War II. The message is simple: focus on doing what is right and honorable, and teach that to future generations of the family, so that people will remember the family as people you can trust and count on. I have heard these words in my head many times.

"BIRKENHEAD FIRST" (OR THE BIRKENHEAD DRILL)

This is a phrase that both my father and grandfather used to say a lot. The HMS *Birkenhead* was a British ship that sunk in 1845, and it was the first time the order "women and children first" was given. For my entire life, the notion of "women and children first" was repeated in various situations. It instilled in me to this day a belief that the needs of the women and children in your life take priority over not your own personal needs but your personal wants. This especially pertains to the safety of the women and children in your life. In the case of children, it is further extended to "youngest first."

The message of "Birkenhead First" has stuck with me. It is part of the reason, along with my mom's influence, that I tend to default to chivalry, and it is why taking care of my children and the younger generations is a priority.

I had a marketing professor in college who once stated in a lecture that "Women are more important than men." The premise was that women carry the species of Man into the future. If a disease struck Earth and killed all women, humankind would die out within 100 years or so. Conversely, if a disease came to earth that killed all men, humankind would continue to exist. Several women would already be pregnant, and some of those babies would be male, therefore preserving the species of Man once those baby boys reach manhood. It is important that we put women and children first in our society.

AUNT FLORENCE

Aunt Florence was my great aunt. She made a sacrifice on behalf of her current and future family that I will never forget. During the Great Depression, when work was tough to find, my Aunt Florence convinced an employer to give her a wage-less job until the business could afford to pay her. There were many who made similar sacrifices during that time just to get by. While I can never accurately measure the impact her decision had on the family, I recognize the selflessness of her efforts and the fact that she helped keep the family afloat financially once she did get paid. She helped pave my father's future and therefore, mine.

It's inspiring to hear stories about family members who sacrificed themselves for the betterment of their family, those who went beyond the call to enable a better future for their family. Many of these people may be members of our armed forces who died in faraway lands for our country. If your family has an Aunt Florence, find her! Capture and tell her story! Thank her if she's still alive. Tell her story, so everyone in the family can remember her sacrifice and the impact she had on their lives.

Legacy is more than just material possessions and assets that are handed down after someone is gone. Legacy is about memories. Legacy is about love of family.

There are many moving pieces in the world that we all must navigate and that our ancestors have had to navigate. Every decision we make not only impacts ourselves, but our families and future generations. Our decisions have an impact on others whose lives we touch and vice versa. What difficulties needed to be overcome for you to even exist in this moment, let alone thrive? How many love stories, goals, future plans, etc. were decided upon, and how many large and small actions were taken by our ancestors for us to inherit the world we have? What sacrifices were made by family members you will never meet that have enabled a path forward for you? Let's honor the sacrifices of those who came before us by creating a world based on peace, love, and mutual respect. Let's get back to our positive foundations. Let's all go out there and be candles. No darkness can extinguish that light.

LOOK UP! LOOK INWARD! What are some of your core values, and where did they come from?

LOOK AROUND! Who in your family can you connect with to share stories and photos of your family and ancestors?

LOOK AHEAD! What types of stories do you want to write to those who will follow you in the generations to come?

CHAPTER 10

HOME

"The strength of a nation derives from the
integrity of the home."

—Confucius

"Home isn't where you're from, it's where you find
light when all grows dark."

—Pierce Brown, Author

Home is where the heart is.

A home is different from a house.

A house is a building.

A home is a safe place filled with love.

T.S. Eliot once said, "Home is where one starts from."

There is something about going home, whether it be coming home each evening from a hard day's work, coming home from a long trip, coming home from college, or a soldier coming home from deployment. There is a familiar, calming feeling when you come home. There is an old adage that states, "you can always go home." For some people, that is not true. Maybe they don't have a home, or they have a split home due to divorce, or they are estranged from their family. I don't know all the details of these types of situations, but if you feel safe trying, I encourage you to reach out to your loved ones, find mutual forgiveness and changed hearts, and try to go home. Home is so important to a happy life.

I travel both domestically and internationally, and international travel always has a different feel to it. While it can be exciting and exotic, I always feel a bit homesick when I am so far away in a foreign land. While our country may not be perfect, it has many freedoms, conveniences, and advantages, like cheeseburgers. Whenever I returned from an international trip, the first thing I did after going home to see the kids was to get a cheeseburger. Yes, the food in other countries is great, but finding a good cheeseburger can be a challenge in certain countries.

While I can feel at home in different cities or countries, it is still not my home. Travel is exciting, but that excitement wears off, and home calls to you. I hated leaving my kids for days or weeks at a time when they were little. The countdown to returning began as soon as my car pulled away from the house. I loved the feeling of coming home to them. The anticipation of seeing loved ones as the plane made the final approach to the airport, and then finally touched down on the runway. The safe feeling of being back on U.S. soil and then catching a glimpse of the U.S. flag made me excited to be back home. Home to cheeseburgers, baseball, football, music, and culture. Home to my family. Home to my pets. Home to my own bed, my own couch, my own TV. Home!

A family friend, Father James Mifsud, was a Catholic priest who was a missionary in Korea during the 1960's and 1970's, helping the country heal after the horrors of the Korean War. Father Jim saw poverty and struggles, but he brought joy and hope to thousands as they tried to rebuild their war-torn country. Father Jim had a personalized license plate that read "USA HOME." I think about Father Jim and that plate every time I return from an international trip. Home is where the heart is. Home is a safe place filled with love and memories.

"Home is where the heart can laugh without shyness. Home is where the heart's tears can dry at their own pace."

— Vernon Baker, Author

"I think that when you invite people to your home, you invite them to yourself."

— Oprah Winfrey

"You can have more than one home. You can carry your roots with you and decide where they grow."

— Henning Monkell, Writer

TOM-ISM: "No matter where you are, you can always go home to God!"

LOOK UP! Where do you feel at home? Go there often!

LOOK AROUND! How can you make others feel at home, especially if they are looking for one?

LOOK AHEAD! We live in a great, but imperfect country... and we are lucky to be citizens of it! What do we improve and prepare our country for the future?

CHAPTER 11

I.C.F.B.

I.C.F.B. It is a very exclusive club. There were ten original members: one founder and nine club members. The club was started by my grandfather, A. Grant Campbell, as a way of making our first visit to him in Philadelphia uniquely memorable.

I.C.F.B. was more than just a club. It was a lifetime memory. It was a bonding experience that became something even more special. It was a memory that turned into a family tradition. Family traditions and memories are critically important. They give us stories to share with each other and pass down to future generations. These types of memories can also be used to honor the people who invented them after they leave this Earth, so that their lineage can learn something about them and share in their love even after they have passed. It is a way to keep the memories of special people alive.

So, what is I.C.F.B.? I.C.F.B. stands for "Ice Cream For Breakfast." My brothers, my Campbell cousins, and I are the original 9 members, and Pop was the founder. My younger brother and my sister would become members later. Shortly after our arrival at my grandparents' house, my brothers and I were ushered into a "top secret" meeting that my parents definitely knew about. (My mom later told me that she wanted to go as well, but she was not allowed!) Pop told us that we were joining a secret club and that members of this club would get ice cream for breakfast every day we were at his house.

Where do I sign?!!!

To make everything official, Pop took some address labels and wrote our names in one corner and the initials I. C. F. B. down the center of the label. These were our official badges. The next morning, he made a big deal about telling our parents that we were going for a walk. He walked us across the street to a su-permarket and strip mall. I don't remember what store we went into or why it was serving ice cream in the morning, but we eagerly went with him to officially become members of the club. It is quite possible that our morning visits were pre-arranged with the shop owner so he would let us in early. We returned to the house victorious, with my parents playing right along with the gimmick.

Pop's birthday is September 16th. Once I had my own kids, I told them about Pop. We honor him on his birthday every year with our own version of the I.C.F.B. Club. While there are no address labels, every September 16th is commemorated with ice cream for breakfast. My kids loved it! As kids get older, it is tougher to keep the magic of these things alive, but I do make it a point to call and remind them to have ice cream for breakfast every September 16th, as I continue to do. It is important to me that I keep Pop's memory alive as long as possible and to honor all he did for me and my family through my dad. I hope that when my kids have their own families, they will re-awaken the tradition. If not, I will!

Ice Cream For Breakfast. I.C.F.B.

I am proud to be a lifelong member! It is a testament to simpler times and to what a vivid imagination, a lot of love, and an ad-dress label with some letters written on it can do to make chil-dren laugh, smile, and carry memories to a legacy. I still have that address label with those precious initials written on it! I recently found it in a lock box where I keep important family documents, which shows you the level of importance it has in my life. I smile every time I think about it.

I smiled again recently when I saw a sign at a Jeni's Ice Cream store in southern California that advertised "Ice Cream For Breakfast" and offered a menu. There was no special membership club, though, and no handwritten address labels as membership badges. I may actually go back to that store on September 16th and place an order! I might even wear my I.C.F.B. badge and see if anyone asks what it means.

Look at the lasting impression that a simple, but unique idea had on a family and future generations of that family. The ice cream couldn't have cost that much, and the homemade name badges certainly are not that expensive. It doesn't take much to make a lasting memory: just a little love and a fun experience.

Think about a simple idea that you could share with your family to make similar memories and leave a similar legacy. These are the things that matter. These are the things that end up being etched in our memories.

LOOK UP! Your legacy is tied to memories that carry on into the future through family stories, not just from the financial assets you leave behind. What can you do today to create a generational memory for your family?

LOOK AROUND! Who are the people you need to form secret clubs with to create lasting memories?

LOOK AHEAD! How can you honor someone from your past by marking something special about them to tell future generations?

KEEP GOING! What memories are you creating for your friends and family to remember you by?

CHAPTER 12

TYPES OF LOVE

"What is love? The person you miss the most
when everyone is around."

—Unknown

"When you love, you open your life to another. All your barriers
are down. Your protective distances collapse. This person is
given absolute permission to come into the deepest temple
of your spirit. Your presence and life can become this person's
ground. It takes courage to let someone so close."

—John O'Donohue

I think we can all agree that we need more love in the world, so it is important to study Love in more detail.

In researching the topic of love, you will find a variety of opinions on how many types of love exist. Some say there are four types. Others say eight, and still, others say something in between. The ancient Greeks identified seven types of love. I will introduce all seven types but focus on one type of love in particular: Agape Love.

1. EROS:　　　　Romantic, passionate love.

2. PHILIA:　　　Affectionate, friendly love.

3. STORGE:　　　Unconditional, familial love.

4.   AGAPE: Selfless, universal love. An empathetic love for God, Nature and our fellow Men.

5.   LUDUS: Playful, flirtatious love.

6.   PRAGMA: Committed, long-lasting love.

7.   PHILAUTIA: Self-love.

I believe Agape love is described as follows in the Bible:

Love is patient and kind,

Love does not envy or boast,

It is not arrogant or rude.

It does not insist on its own way,

It is not irritable or resentful,

It does not rejoice at wrongdoing but rejoices with the truth.

Love bears all things, believes all things, hopes all things, endures all things.

(1 Corinthians 13:4 – 7)

Agape love is often considered the purest and deepest form of love. It is said to be the form of love that God has for his children. It is a selfless, unconditional love focused on providing compassion, support, and joy to others. It is essentially "Loving for the sake of Love," (kind of a Tom-ism!)

If Agape love is indeed defined accurately in Corinthians 13:4-7, then it would follow that the characteristics of Agape love are:

Patience

Kindness

Selflessness

Honesty

Integrity

Empathy

Humility

Generosity

Forgiving

Faithful

Remember, Agape love isn't about perfection but about genuine caring, selflessness, and unwavering support for those you love. Practice it daily, and watch your relationships flourish. It's an awareness to do your best to love people the way that they need to be loved.

If you practice Agape love, you will try to put the needs of others first and serve others selflessly. This doesn't mean you should neglect your own needs or de-prioritize your importance in the relationship. It doesn't mean that you need to say yes to everything. Healthy boundaries are still required. What it does mean is to have an awareness of the needs of others around you and the compassion to do what you can to help and support them.

Agape love is difficult. It takes strength. It takes faith. It takes a tremendous amount of self-love. Agape love can empty you, so you need to know how to fill yourself back up. Agape love is giving without expectation of anything in return, which can be a challenge for any of us.

Agape love can also feel overwhelming to the recipient. They may not be used to being treated this way. It is important, as in all relationships, to have open and honest communication and to understand and respect boundaries when it comes to love and how recipients wish to be loved. Again, the goal is to love someone the way they need and want to be loved. You can still love them the way you want to love them, but it must be comfortable for them as well.

If we do our best to love one another, this love will multiply. It will not only go viral, as they say, but it will also go exponential. We should try to show Agape love where we can. If we decide to do our best to approach the world in this way, we will touch lives in ways that we will never know or see. We will create loving experiences and memories for people that are both close to us and even for those who we randomly encounter every day. As Bob Goff says, "Love isn't something we fall into, love is someone we become."

"Agape love says, 'I love you because I choose to love you.'
It loves without consideration of personal
cost or reciprocation."

— Unknown

"I don't have time to worry about who doesn't like me. I am too busy loving the people who love me."

— Unknown

"Unable are the Loved to die, For Love is immortality."

— Emily Dickinson

"In the evening of life, we will be judged on love alone."

— St. John of the Cross

I usually end each chapter with a Tom-ism or a call to action tied to the *Gotta Look Up* brand and mission. But this time, rather than inviting you to Look Up, I invite you to LOVE UP! Open your hearts! Ask that special person out! Get to know a friend on a deeper level. Reach out to that family member. Call someone who might be alone. Hold the door open for someone. Share a smile with a stranger. Try your best to approach things with Agape love. As fallible human beings, we will never get Agape love perfect, but we can improve the world by attempting to do it to the best of our abilities and by making our best effort to apply its principles!

LOOK UP! and **LOVE UP!** Tell someone you love them! Let them know how you feel while you're both still here!

Let me end this chapter by sharing some of the greatest words ever spoken. Words of advice that we can all use every day. The 11th Commandment from Jesus Christ:

"Love one another as I have loved you."

LOOK AROUND! IMPROVE YOUR WORLD

CHAPTER 13

GET OUT OF THE QUICKSAND!

"Ships don't sink because of the water around them. Ships sink because of the water that gets in them. Don't let what's happening around you get inside you and weigh you down."

—Unknown

Quicksand struck fear in me as a child. Getting stuck and sinking in quicksand was the worst fate I could imagine. I was first introduced to quicksand while watching the *Tarzan* television series starring Ron Ely. In the show, quicksand was something to be feared because whenever someone fell into it, they invariably struggled, thrashed about, and therefore sank and drowned. Everyone, that is, except for Tarzan. Tarzan had help. He would either call on a chimpanzee to throw him a rope or a convenient vine located nearby, or he would call an elephant to come over and extend a trunk to pull him out. Or, as my dad used to tell me, "Don't worry, the cameraman is there."

As a kid, I was scared to death of quicksand. Of course, as kids our imaginations would run wild, and we would create games where the floor was either lava or quicksand. So, obviously we would use the furniture to avoid it and leave shoe prints on various cushions and throw pillows, much to my mom's delight.

As an adult, I would come to define quicksand as any emotional struggle, whether of my own doing or brought into my life by others. You learn that various forms of quicksand become part of your daily life. Negativity is quicksand. Focusing on revenge is quicksand. A bad relationship or a divorce is quicksand. Loneliness is quicksand. Lies and deceit are quicksand. A dead-end job or a bad boss is quicksand. Financial debt is quicksand. Lack of purpose is quicksand.

One of the influencers I follow on social media is Ed Mylett. One of the principles that Ed likes to state goes something like this: "we are most qualified to help those who are where we once were." So, when people come to me for advice on how to deal with divorce or some other personal challenge, the first thing I make sure of is that they are safe. The second thing that I tell them is to make sure that they get out of, and stay out of, the quicksand. It is critically important to recognize all forms of quicksand as soon as possible and stop thrashing about so as not to sink. The best way out of quicksand is to remain calm and be logical and deliberate.

I've been to the abyss. I've been in the quicksand. When you're in the middle of the quicksand, it is only human and natural to want to lash out, to seek revenge, to win. But when you're in quicksand, the only winning is to get out of it as fast as you can.

So, how do you get out of quicksand? I'm going to tell you what I did, and, unlike Tarzan, I did it without a loin cloth, a chimpanzee, or an elephant.

The best way out of quicksand is to calm yourself down, create stillness and quiet, and slowly pull yourself out of the muck and the mire by finding what I call our "Trees of Joy."

TREES OF JOY

> "The best time to plant a tree was 20 years ago,
> the second-best time is today."
>
> —Ancient Chinese Proverb

> "There is nothing wrong with having a tree as a friend."
>
> —Bob Ross, Painter

Trees of Joy are the things that make you most happy at a core level. Trees of Joy are the things that you can throw a rope around to help pull you out of your quicksand.

For me to get out of my quicksand, I had to look back into my past. I had to look at the things that brought me joy in my childhood, as well as in my adult life. First and foremost, my kids brought me joy. But the quicksand I found myself in was primarily caused by my estrangement from them. So, I had to find other Trees of Joy. To do that, I looked back to my childhood and listed my favorite things. (Don't worry, I won't sing the song from "The Sound of Music...." And I apologize to everyone who now has that song playing on a loop in their heads).

What were those favorite things that became my Trees of Joy?

→ God, Jesus, and Faith
→ Family
→ Friends
→ Animals, particularly elephants
→ Nature, hiking, walking on the beach
→ Sports
→ Writing
→ Reading about history, particularly World War II

So, I spent more time pursuing those interests that brought me more joy and distracted me from the quicksand. More joy brought more strength and confidence, made me a better man, and allowed me to go back into the quicksand to help my kids deal with, and get out of, their quicksand.

"Hope is important because it can make the present moment less difficult to bear. If we believe that tomorrow will be better, we can bear a hardship today."

— Thich Nhat Hanh

"I like to envision the whole world as a jigsaw puzzle...If you look at the whole picture, it is overwhelming and terrifying, but if you work on your little part and know that people all over the world are working on their little bits, that's what gives you hope."

— Jane Goodall

Trees of Joy can also be people you know, like family and close friends. People who you can count on to take your rope and hold it tight to help you climb out of the quicksand.

"I see people, but they look like trees..." From the Blind Man Gospel (Mark 8:24)

To get started on a list of your own Trees of Joy, ask yourself these questions:

1. What do you love?

2. Who do you love?

3. Where do you find happiness?

4. Who are your "go to" people?

5. What do you believe spiritually?

<u>NOTE</u>: A couple of key points to stress here.

1. While people can certainly be your "trees," do not count on other people to be the ones who pull you out of your quicksand. Only you can do that! Maybe with their support and help, but you have to be the one to pull!

2. Make sure your "trees" are legal and do not involve drugs, other substances, or behaviors that can get you into far worse and deeper quicksand.

Trees of Joy are more focused in the present. You use them to get out of the quicksand right now! While we may identify our Trees of Joy from our past, they are used in the present to pull us out of the quicksand. Once you've successfully used your Trees of Joy to get out of the quicksand, you can then look toward the future by finding "Anchors of Hope" to identify new goals, hopes, dreams, and even a renewed and powerful purpose.

ANCHORS OF HOPE

"A ship in harbor is safe, but that's not what ships are built for."

—John A. Shedd, American Author and Professor

"Hope is an anchor for the soul ."

—Hebrews 6:19

"Sometimes you have to let go of the picture of what you thought it would be like and learn to find joy in the story you are actually living."

—Rachel Marie Martin

"Let us confidently hope that all will yet be well."

—Abraham Lincoln

What are Anchors of Hope? Let's first focus on what an anchor is and its purpose. Anchors are used by ships to keep them from drifting off in the current. Anchors are used to secure pictures and artwork to the wall. Anchors are things that tie us to a foundation. Anchors are a Christian symbol of hope. Anchors represent hope for a new future, new decisions, and new journeys, but they can always be used to secure us to a foundation when the going gets tough.

An Anchor of Hope can be anything in our life that grounds us in self-confidence, happiness, or security. Our Anchors of Hope give us the proper perspective when dealing with temporary negativity in our lives. These Anchors can also allow us to venture back into the quicksand when needed and allow us to pull ourselves out by the rope when we are done.

Anchors of Hope are keys to a better, happier future. They are our dreams, goals, objectives, and purpose. They allow us to focus our attention and energy toward improving our lives. Some of my Anchors of Hope are:

1. God & Spirituality

2. Family & Children

3. Nature

4. Friends

5. Purpose

6. Exercise & Physical health

7. Mental health

8. Better career path

9. Better relationships

    10. Self-care

    11. Truth

    12. Personal growth

    13. Financial health

    14. Travel

Anchors of Hope represent positive change for your life, health, and spirit. They give you the confidence to go back into the quicksand at any time to help others get out. As Fyodor Dostoevsky once said, "To live without hope is to cease to live."

Hope is a foundation upon which we can build a future. Hope points us to better tomorrows. Hope encourages us to take action and keep going. As Christopher Reeve once said, "Once you choose hope, anything is possible." He went from A-List actor to quadriplegic after a horse jumping accident. He never gave up. He persisted. He continued to have hope and inspired many people to do the same.

Bishop Desmond Tutu described hope as, "Being able to see that there is light despite all of the darkness." Sometimes it is difficult to see that light, but if you find yourself lost or in a desperate time, friends and family can provide enough light to get you through until you can shine on your own.

TOM-ISM:
"A hand is always stronger when it holds another.
Arms are always stronger when they embrace.
Shoulders are always stronger when they carry a child.
A mind is always stronger when it thinks of others.
A heart is always stronger when it loves unconditionally."

LOOK UP! Find your Trees of Joy! Keep yourself and others out of the quicksand!

LOOK AROUND! Who needs you to throw them a rope to help pull them out of their quicksand?

LOOK AHEAD! What are your future dreams for your life that you can use as Anchors of Hope?

KEEP GOING! Where will your ship take you next?

CHAPTER 14

FLYOVER COUNTRY?...
HARDLY!

"Let us at all times remember that all American citizens are brothers of a common country and should dwell together in the bonds of fraternal feeling."

—Abraham Lincoln

"To become truly great, one has to stand with people, not above them."

—Montesquieu

I recently had the pleasure of experiencing what I call "windscreen time." What we call a windshield in the U.S., the Brits call a windscreen.

While *Gotta Look Up* advocates for reducing screen time, I think windscreen time is a great alternative. If we spend time looking through our windscreens, that means we are going somewhere, we are seeing things, learning new things, and exploring the world around us. And you'd better not be texting on that other screen while you're experiencing windscreen time!

I recently spent four days on the road with my son, driving with him from San Jose, California to Kansas City, Missouri where he attended fixed-wing flight school to pursue his dreams. It is a long haul but a tremendous bonding experience. We talked about a lot...past, present, and future; the good, bad, and ugly.

We covered some difficult topics and developed a deeper understanding of each other as a result. I learned a lot about the man my son has become, and I am very proud of him.

I also learned a lot about myself. I learned that I have been, and still am, a pretty good dad. I learned that my kids care about me and want me to pursue my happiness.

And I learned a lot about my country. There is a whole lot of nothing out there...which gave me time to think about everything.

Many people on the coasts of this country refer to the area that we covered on this drive as "flyover country." And while that name might describe it from one perspective, it falls well short of an accurate description.

You see, within what many call "flyover country" live people that work in foundational industries, on top of which their fellow coastal citizens build their lives. I saw farms, ranches, and energy production facilities, without which this country could not run, could not feed itself, and could not prosper. I saw many trucks and truckers, without whom, commerce in this country would come to a standstill.

Driving all that way, spanning just over half of the country, I developed a newfound respect for our truckers...even though one of them didn't check his blind spot and almost took us out!

So, I will no longer refer to the middle part of my country as "flyover country" because that would mean that my fellow citizens who live in these areas would be "flyover people," and they deserve more respect than that moniker affords. They are critical cogs in our machine and the backbone of this country.

GOTTA LOOK UP... TO THEM!

"Treating everyone as important and showing respect is not that hard. Just put yourself in other people's shoes and give them the respect and courtesy that you would like to receive."

— Tony Dungy

"There are people you meet who become impossible to forget. They were not sent to you by accident, but instead, destined to open a doorway to a different version of your life."

— Erin Matlock

CHAPTER 15

BAGS OF CANDY

"There can be no greater gift than that of giving one's time and energy to help others without expecting anything in return."

—Nelson Mandela

"To make a difference in someone's life you don't have to be rich, beautiful, or perfect. You just have to care."

—Mandy Hale

I have a new favorite hobby, taught to me by a friend and mentor, Marty Melville. Marty stood by me and supported me during a very difficult time in my career. Sadly, Marty is no longer with us; he left us way too soon.

I was on a business trip with Marty when he made a beeline for the airport gift shop. He bought a couple of candy bars and a bag of treats. I asked him, half-jokingly, how he planned to eat all of that on a one-hour flight. "This isn't for me," he said. "You'll see."

On the jetway, about to enter the plane, he pulled out the bag full of treats, handed them to the flight attendant at the door and said, "These are for you." She smiled very wide and thanked him profusely. The joy on her face was palpable. This small, thoughtful gesture had made her day.

When Marty and I got to our aisle seats across from each other, I told him that it was a good thing he did and that he made that lady's day. He told me that flight attendants put up with a lot of crap. This was a small way to show appreciation for what they do and to help put smiles on their faces. I found a new level of respect for Marty that day. I also learned that the flight attendant offered him a free drink, which I'm guessing was a planned side benefit.

As my business travel has increased, this memory of Marty giving candy to the flight attendants has rushed forward in my mind. I decided to keep Marty's tradition going, and I have fun bringing smiles to the flight crews on all of my flights. So far, so good! It is a lot of fun to see the reactions! And yes, I have been offered free drinks on pretty much every flight. I am not a drinker though, so they usually default to an extra bag of snacks or cookies, which is good enough for me.

We can apply this same giving spirit of "Bags of Candy" without ever boarding a flight. We can surprise people on bridges or toll roads by paying for the car behind us. We can donate food or items of clothing to families in need. We can donate bags of food or toys to animal shelters or spend time giving some love to the dogs and cats there if we can't take them home. "Bags of Candy" is more of an approach to life rather than a specific action. It is finding the gaps in society where we can contribute a little bit of love and caring to fill the void.

On a recent flight, I actually had a flight attendant call me the "candy man." I enjoy being the candy man! Instead of a sugar rush from eating the bags of candy, I get the "love rush" that comes with putting a smile on someone else's face.

LOOK UP! Who is no longer with us but had an impact on your life? How can you honor them through how you live your life?

LOOK AROUND! Who can you share a bag of candy with to help cover the world with chocolate and a miracle or two?

LOOK AHEAD! What passions do you have in life where you can make the concept of "Bags of Candy" part of your brand?

THE YELLOW ROSE

"The flower does not dream of the bee.
It blossoms and the bee comes."

—Mark Nepo

"The sun does not shine for a few trees and flowers,
but for the wide world's joy."

—Henry Ward Beecher

"When you like a flower, you just pluck it. But when you love a flower, you water it daily...!"

One who understands this, understands life...

— Buddha

Anyone who has experienced divorce knows the negative impact it has on the kids, regardless of their age. The stability of their lives is uprooted, and they are forced to navigate separated parents and extended families. It becomes extremely difficult for the kids when the parents and extended families cannot move forward amicably and feel like they need to give their opinions or even lie about the other parent.

Such is the background for this story. While I won't get into all the negative details, let's just say that my kids were fed non-truths that had a negative impact on their relationship with me, especially my daughter. My daughter would not speak to me for about a year. The only way I got to see her during that time was to volunteer for lunch duty at her school. So, I did. As much as I could. Slowly but surely, she went from ignoring me, to waving to me, to coming into my line...especially when mashed potatoes were being served.

You see, when both kids were little, whenever we had mashed potatoes for dinner at home, but especially at Thanksgiving, I would form a volcano out of the mashed potatoes and make a well for the gravy, which was the lava of course.

Mashed potato volcanoes helped me get my daughter back. When she finally came into my line, I made her one and got a smile. The next time mashed potatoes were being served, she came back to my line, and I made her another volcano. This time her friend asked for one too. And on future occasions when mashed potatoes were being served, more and more of her friends would ask for a volcano, and everyone who asked, got one.

It was during this same year that my daughter was applying to high schools. She had her heart set on a particular private Catholic high school that her closest friends were applying to as well. I was not involved in her original application process as she wasn't speaking with me at that time. She did not get accepted. It was very upsetting for her to watch her friends get accepted and attend while she went to a different school with her brother and no other familiar faces.

Sophomore year, she reapplied, this time with my support and involvement. The admissions office had some concerns about her math grades and whether she could keep up with the math workload at the school. I convinced them not to judge her by a piece of paper, but to talk to her in person. I got them to agree to meet with my daughter for a face-to-face interview, which they don't normally do. This time she got in!

Now the challenge was finding a way to pay for her tuition while managing a divorce, mounting legal fees, and no financial assistance from anyone else. She told me she could work off a portion of her tuition, and she would do whatever it took to help so she could attend that school. I told her we would find a way, just the two of us, if necessary. My only requirements were that she work hard, get good grades, and get involved at the school through sports, clubs, and social activities and not just go home after class. She kept up her end of that bargain, though I do believe that her way of working off her tuition by volunteering as a member of the sports medicine team was more of a way to meet boys than anything else. She got amazing grades, including straight A's many times, and made the Dean's list. She joined the women's diving team because it was one of two "no cut" sports, and she didn't want to do cross country running. She got involved in school volunteer work and social clubs. I did my part through financial gymnastics, well-timed commission checks, and by living off either peanut butter sandwiches or bean burritos until the next paycheck hit. This high school experience transformed her into a confident young woman and was worth every penny of the money, the sacrifice, and the hard work that she and I put in as a team. Funny side note, she got fantastic grades in math. Her worst grades were in religion!

You might be asking, "Yeah, but what does this have to do with a yellow rose?" I'm getting to that! This high school's colors are black and gold. Unbeknownst to me, they give the graduating students a single yellow rose to give to their parents at the baccalaureate celebration the day before graduation. A baccalaureate service is sort of a farewell ceremony for senior students who are graduating high school or college. Given I knew what she and I went through to get her to this point, I was not going to miss any of it, and I was going to get the best seat in the house for both the baccalaureate and the graduation ceremony the next day. I got there an hour early and took a seat near the front on the aisle where I knew she would be walking, so I could see her come in. As people started filing into the event, I noticed some storm clouds starting to form.

The event starts, and the kids proceed to their seats. I see my girl, and we smile at each other as she walks past. Now a confident young woman.

Fast forward through the baccalaureate where we get to the part when the celebrant announces that the seniors will now take a single yellow rose to give to their parents. Right after that announcement, her mom suddenly appeared next to me. I pointed over to where our daughter was and said, "She's over there looking for you." Her mom left to go find her to get the rose while I stood there alone, thinking about what it took to get to this point, the sacrifices made that no one else knew about, including my daughter. I watched happy families and parents getting their roses from their kids. Then, something told me to turn around. When I did, I saw my beautiful, smart, and talented girl hand her mom the rose. My daughter then turned and made her way toward me with a big smile on her face... extending a second yellow rose out to me! Somehow, she was able to get a second one! Somehow, she made sure to honor me. It is, to this day, the most beautiful flower I have ever seen. I gave her a hug and held that rose tight in my hand as she went back to her seat.

Those storm clouds erupted and rained down on the crowd, sending well-dressed parents and grandparents scurrying for cover. I just sat in my seat in the rain, clutching a yellow rose that meant so much to me, watching the kids delight in getting drenched, and sharing my own tears of joy with those of the heavens that were falling on all of us...as a double rainbow appeared in the distance.

The most beautiful flower I've ever seen.

LOOK UP! You never know how and when the Universe will conspire to honor your efforts!

LOOK AROUND! Are you taking cover or sitting in the rain with a smile on your face?

LOOK AROUND! Who might be bringing you an unexpected "yellow rose?"

KEEP GOING! If you're in a tough spot, things will get better.

CHAPTER 17

KINTSUGI

"Your job is to lift the fallen, restore the broken,
and heal the hurting."

—Joel Osteen

"Always leave people better than you found them. Hug the
hurt. Kiss the broken. Befriend the lost. Love the lonely."

—Unknown

We've all had trials and tribulations. Good and bad relationships. Successes and failures. We are all broken in some way. The key is how we handle these breaks and how we recover. The Japanese concept of "kintsugi" is a beautiful way of healing broken parts.

Kintsugi means "golden joinery." It comes from the root "kintsukuroi" which means "golden repair."

Kintsugi is the Japanese art of repairing broken pottery by mending the areas of breakage with lacquer, dusted or mixed with powdered gold, silver, or platinum.

As a philosophy, kintsugi treats breakage and repair as part of the history of an object rather than something to disguise.

Kintsugi teaches us to accept fragility, build strength and resilience, and to take pride in the imperfect. Our brokenness is what makes us human. It makes us authentic. It allows us to bond with others who experience similar challenges and breakages. Kintsugi shows us the value and beauty in repairing our broken parts and in learning and growing from our mistakes The use of precious metals to make the repairs under kintsugi is not lost on me. Our broken pieces represent our experiences and learnings. The golden repair in our lives comes from the help and love of our family, our friends, and our God. We will continue to break, repair, and move forward with our lives. There is beauty in our brokenness and in our courage to learn, improve, love, forgive, and keep going.

We are all broken in some way, but if we look at our scars and breaks through the lenses of kintsugi, breaks become golden repairs, badges of honor, and part of the quilt of our lives.

Many of us may feel more broken when relationships end or when important people in our lives evolve and move on in different directions. We might feel lost, broken, or even a bit stupid for having high expectations for the relationship. I don't believe it is ever wrong to love someone who may feel broken or to love someone who needs our genuine love and friendship to see their value, to find the light within themselves, and to pursue their happiness and become who they are supposed to be.

While we may feel broken in the short term, the golden lacquer of time will help us heal that break and make us proud for daring to love someone.

We are all miracles and works of art, divinely created. We are all broken in some way, but we can repair each other and lift each other up with love, forgiveness, kindness, respect, and understanding.

"It is easier to build strong children than to repair broken men."

— Frederick Douglas

"Mosaics are made from broken pieces, but they're still a work of art. And so are you."

— Unknown

TOM-ISM: "We are all broken in some way. I am broken too. But I will break off a piece of my heart…a piece of me, and I will give it to you…to help make you whole."

LOOK UP! Where are you broken and in need of repair?

LOOK AROUND! Who do you know that may also be broken and in need of your help? Be the missing piece, or the gold lacquer, in someone's life to help make them whole!

KEEP GOING! We are all works of art, walking mosaics made up of broken and repaired pieces that we collect throughout our lives.

CHAPTER 18

HUGS

"A hug is always the right size."

— Winnie The Pooh

"Hugs matter! One hug from the right person
takes all your stress away."

— Unknown

Hugs are great! Hugs are a genuine display of affection that can range from familial to friendly to deeply intimate. Hugs are an amazing exchange of energy where two people become one for a brief moment in time, or even better, an extended period of time (with proper consent as always, of course!).

Hugs are powerful! They show someone we care. They are an exchange of energy between two or more people. They give us warmth, both physical and spiritual, and usually all parties benefit from the exchange.

A hug is an expression of caring that does not require any words. You can feel the words in each hug. Hugs are an expression of:

→ A bond
→ Caring
→ Family
→ Friendship
→ Love
→ Teamwork

→ Comfort
→ Safety
→ Magic

"Hugs are so underrated.
Hugs are a most beautiful form of communication that allows
the other person to know beyond a doubt that they matter.
Sometimes, we don't need any advice, just a
hug to make you feel better.
There's more power in a good hug than any words combined.
Hugs are the most healing thing ever."

— Unknown

Hugs are two souls connecting their energy through an embrace of physical bodies. If the act of hugging is driven by our souls, then isn't it possible that hugs can be delivered from beyond? Can our loved ones still hug us after they have passed and crossed over? Are the shivers and goosebumps we get on occasion actually a spiritual hug from a loved one in another dimension?

Rosa Perry once said, "I just hugged you in my thoughts. I hope you felt it." I love this sentiment! How many people do you hug in your thoughts every day? And while I am more of an advocate for hugs in person, if you can only send a text with a hug emoji to someone who needs it, by all means, do it!

When is the last time you were held by someone? Not one of those quick obligatory hugs, but truly held by someone you care about. Held in a way that makes the rest of the world seem to disappear? Hug like that!

Hugs! Use them often!

"The best thing to hold onto in life is each other."
— Audrey Hepburn

"After going through what he'd been through, he was praised for being tough, but what he really wanted was to be held and loved."

— Samantha Camargo

"I need a hug.
Not the regular two seconds hug.
The warm sunset kind of hug.
The body crushing, 'I see you' kind of hug.
The type that leaves you feeling ten times
lighter than your actual weight.
The type that fixes the cracks in your bones, and
the bruises in your heart.
The kind that whispers, 'It's alright, I'm here,
I understand, and I'm not letting go.'
That's the kind of hug I need."

— Unknown

TOM-ISM: "The internet can't hug you back."

LOOK UP! Who needs a hug right now? Who do you need a hug from? Get their permission first!

LOOK AHEAD! Find someone huggable and give them one! Get their permission first!

LOOK AHEAD! Keep Hugging!

CHAPTER 19

SGT DEXTER WILSON FINCHER

Sgt. Dexter Wilson Fincher is a man I never met. I had never heard of him until December 7th, 2021.

I have always had an interest in and affinity for history, particularly World War II. I study it because I want to understand the conditions and mentality that leads to tyranny so we can see the patterns well in advance and prevent similar tragedies from taking shape.

I had always wanted to go to Pearl Harbor for the anniversary of the attack. So, I cashed in some air miles and went. I was fortunate to meet a couple of veterans who were there that day, including 100-year-old Mr. Higgins, who was stationed on Ford Island and was there during the attack. As I always do when I see a World War II veteran, I thanked Mr. Higgins and his buddies for their service and for giving me the opportunity to live and raise my family in freedom and prosperity.

I was fortunate enough to get a ticket to go to the USS *Arizona* Memorial. I was in one of the tour groups allowed to visit after the main commemoration and ceremony in the early morning hours, at the actual time of the attack 80 years prior.

When I arrived at the USS *Arizona* Memorial, we were told to keep moving, as we only had ten minutes on the memorial ship. The crowd slowly flowed to the back of the memorial to see the list of names of those who perished 80 years ago, plus the names of those who survived that day, lived fruitful lives, and chose to be buried at sea with their shipmates. As I made my way back toward the dock to catch the launch back to the visitors' center, I noticed a park ranger standing next to a table with two baskets sitting on top of it. In one basket were flower petals from Hawaiian leis. The second basket contained small pieces of paper with the names of the heroes who perished that day. Guests were invited to pick a name and a flower petal and toss them into the water as a tribute to the person whose name was picked. I picked Sgt. Dexter Wilson Fincher from the basket.

It is common to see the USS Arizona "cry" or "bleed" drops of oil that escape the ship and rise to the surface…even 80 plus years later. Usually they are small, between 6 inches to a foot in diameter. Right after I dropped the flower petal in the water, a small slick grew larger and larger and created rainbow colors on the water. It was impressive, and I was not the only one who noticed. What was the message being sent? Was it a message of "thanks" from those who we honored in that moment? Was it a message of thanks directed at me specifically for keeping memories alive in a world that is quickly forgetting how close we came to losing everything in World War II? I do not know the exact meaning, but I do know something special happened that day that I will not soon forget.

These are the types of things you see when you take the time to "look up." These are the messages the Universe sends you when you pay attention and keep your mind open. Rest in peace, Sgt. Fincher. I thank you, your shipmates, and your buddies from the greatest generation for all you did. Thank you especially to all of those who, like yourself, paid the ultimate price, allowing us to inherit the world we live in today. We owe it to all of you not to screw things up again.

War is stupid. Stop the hate! Stop the killing! Choose love! Choose peace! Again, I would like to call on all world leaders to:

LOOK UP! From your ego!

LOOK AROUND! At your citizens. Are you serving them and working in their best interests?

LOOK AHEAD! Take actions focused solely on building a prosperous and peaceful future for your citizens! This is what a positive legacy is all about, not conquest and domination, but **LOVE!**

CHAPTER 20

HEROES

"A hero is an ordinary individual who finds the strength to persevere and endure in spite of overwhelming obstacles."

— Christopher Reeve

"A hero is someone who has given his or her life to something bigger than oneself."

— Joseph Campbell

What comes to mind when you hear the word "hero?" Soldiers, firefighters, police officers, healthcare workers? Most of these folks are everyday heroes. Most heroes are courageous and unselfish. I watch the Army-Navy football game every year. It is the one college football game that I make sure to watch. A few years back, I heard someone say something about the game that really struck me. I am paraphrasing, but it went something like this: "The Army-Navy game is the one football game where every player on the field would give up his life for everyone watching in the stands." I do need to add a mention for the Air Force Academy, The Citadel, and other military institutions where these words also apply. In the Bible, John 15:13 tells us that, "Greater love has no one than this: to lay down one's life for one's friends." There are many stories throughout history of people sacrificing their life for the lives of others. Soldiers, firefighters, police officers, organ donors. All heroes.

Who were the heroes in your life? Growing up, mine were mostly athletes and celebrities. People who didn't know that I even existed, but people I would strive to be like and pattern my life after. What I didn't realize was that some of my teachers were going to be the among the greatest heroes in my life when I looked back on the foundation they helped establish and the character they helped develop. I mostly remember my elementary school teachers, Miss Santich and Miss Silva, but the most impactful was Miss Grover, who taught me for three grades and had the largest impact on my success. Take a minute right now to think about the teachers who had the greatest impact on you. How different would your life be without their influence? Good teachers are heroes.

Who are the heroes in your life now? For me, my mom and dad will always be my heroes. They gave me life and made sacrifices that I will never know about to give me the best life they possibly could. I don't think I fully appreciated their heroism until I had kids of my own and experienced the awesome responsibilities that come with the joy and adventure of being a parent. Good parents are the best heroes. Whether it be the single mom or dad that works multiple jobs to keep food on the table and a roof over their family; the mom or dad who takes a second job to pay for their kids' education, birthday, or Christmas presents; the dad who goes into a coal mine every day and takes his kid to a basketball game in his blackened work clothes; the truck drivers who are away from their families for days at a time, ensuring shelves are stocked with essentials; or the volunteers who work at soup kitchens, orphanages, and shelters. Essentially, I believe heroes are the those who put their needs aside to fulfill their responsibilities to their families every day.

"Throughout my life I've met plenty of superheroes, but the strongest and most effective among them were simply human and knew they weren't perfect. They were the men and women who, like my father, believed in their duty to country and sacrificed for others without hesitation."

— Ann E. Dunwoody, Gulf War Veteran
and Medal of Honor winner

TOM-ISM: "You can be a hero without superpowers, tights, or a cape. You just need to care."

LOOK UP! Who are the heroes in your life?

LOOK AHEAD! Who are you a hero for?

LOOK AHEAD! Where can you be a hero or support those who are heroes?

CHAPTER 21

BASEBALL AND "THE ICE CREAM INNING"

"Say hey!"

—Willie Mays

"It's a great day for a ball game, let's play two!"

—Ernie Banks

Baseball has always been an important part of my life. I played little league baseball for three years. My first team was the Oaks, my second team was the Owls, and my third team was the Senators. Our sponsors were local small businesses, advertised on the front of our t-shirts. My favorite players were Reggie Jackson and Campy Campaneris of the Oakland A's.

Baseball was something I could always talk about with my dad. It was the activity we did together on a daily or weekly basis. Playing catch with my dad is such a cherished memory, As I mentioned in an earlier chapter, I still carry a piece of dad's old first baseman's mitt with me on my key chain. My parents were at every little league game they could get to, but between three baseball-playing sons, it was hard to get to our games if played at the same time. I always remember looking up into the stands when I made a good play to see my dad smiling and giving me a thumbs up. Baseball was always our bond. To this day, I will tear up watching the movie *Field of Dreams* because I would give anything to have one more catch with my dad and my brothers.

Later in life, baseball evolved into adult softball leagues. At one point, my three brothers and I were on the same team. My mom and dad came to one of our games, and I think that this game was my dad's favorite game of all time. All four of his boys on the same field, with him probably thinking he should get out there with us because he could still do it. He was an excellent baseball player in his youth and was even approached by a scout from the Chicago Cubs.

When my son was old enough to start T-ball, we signed him up, and I volunteered to be an assistant coach. It was probably more fun for me than for my son, but he liked being around the other kids and put in a good effort. As anyone who has ever coached a kids' sports team will know, it is difficult to keep them focused on things at an early age.

After a couple of years, the boys are moved from hitting the ball off a tee to "coach pitch," where the coaches "soft toss" pitches into their own batters. At this level, each team bats until they either get out three times or bat through the order.

As we moved slowly through one of the games, I decided to give the kids a little extra incentive. I called them all over for a quick team meeting before taking the field for the next inning. "OK," I said, "here's the deal...if you guys get three outs before they score a run, I'll buy ice cream for the whole team." Incentive. They ran out onto the field more excited than I have ever seen them.

The other team's first batter gets up. He hits an infield ground ball, and he is thrown out. Our team gets more excited.

The second batter comes up. Another infield grounder for an out. Our team gets even more excited!

The next batter...gets a hit and is on base. Our team's excitement comes down a notch and turns to concern.

"Relax out there," I tell them. "Play is at first or second base."

The next batter gets up...and gets on base as well!

"You're alright, guys. Play is at first, second, or third. Whatever is the easy base."

Next batter gets a hit. Now, the bases are loaded, and the kids are worried.

"One more out, gentlemen! Play is at any base. Just focus on making the play."

The next batter hits a slow ground ball to second base.

I watch as our second baseman attacks the ball, picks it up, and starts to shake as he throws it toward first base.

I watch our first baseman, arms outstretched and shaking, as the ball comes toward him in what seemed like slow motion.

He catches the ball!

The runner is out!

3 outs...

Zero runs...

Ice cream!!!

There is bedlam on the field as our kids run off celebrating, hugging, and high fiving like they just won the World Series, all while confused parents on both baselines wonder what the hell just happened.

After the game, we all went to Baskin Robbins. It might have been the best eighty-plus dollars I've ever spent.

Those kids may forget the specific date of that game, and likely the outcome, but they will never forget "The Ice Cream Inning."

TOM-ISM: "To paraphrase the great Chicago Cubs shortstop Ernie Banks, 'It's a great day for a scoop of ice cream, let's get two!'"

LOOK UP! What unique memories can you make for your family?

LOOK AROUND! Do something for kids today that they will always remember and pass along to future generations.

LOOK AHEAD! What would be a good day to add ice cream to your next little league game, or breakfast menu?

CHAPTER 22

PANNING FOR GOLD

"It is health that is real wealth and not
pieces of gold and silver."

—Mahatma Gandhi

"Life is not what you alone make it. Life is the input of
everyone who touched your life and every experience
that entered it. We are all part of one another. "

—Yuri Kochiyama

I've always loved history. I love the stories of ancient cultures, exploration, and treasure hunts. I like learning how landscapes have changed due to war and conquest. One of the chapters of history that most intrigued me was the California Gold Rush. Having lived in California for most of my life, I was keenly interested in learning about John Sutter and his fort and mill just outside of Sacramento, California. James Marshall was the first one credited with discovering gold on Sutter's property, but my guess is that native populations were probably finding nuggets years before it all became documented history.

I was amazed by the stories of people coming from across the United States by covered wagon and other countries by clipper ship via the dangerous ocean passage around Cape Horn. Everyone was looking to make their fortune, though few did.

Most of the people who achieved wealth during the Gold Rush did so by providing the infrastructure, tools, and necessary services to the miners, not the miners themselves. The height of the California Gold Rush took place in 1849. Many of the prospectors who flooded San Francisco to get to the Gold Country were called "Forty-niners" and became the inspiration for naming the pro football team, the San Francisco 49ers.

The Gold Rush is part of the fourth grade curriculum in California schools. As part of this curriculum, many schools will take their fourth grade classes on a field trip to Columbia, California, where students can experience what life was like in an 1849 western town. To top it all off, the kids are given a demonstration and lesson on how to pan for gold, and they are allowed to keep whatever they find!

I was fortunate to have various sales jobs that allowed time off when necessary to join my kids on these types of trips as a parent chaperone. As a history enthusiast, I may have enjoyed these trips more than the kids! I was fortunate to chaperone my daughter's fourth grade trip to the Gold Country! Nothing better than being on a bus for hours on a winding, mountain road with a bunch of car sick kids and a few carsick adults. I was never a Boy Scout, but I was always prepared because my mom taught me well. I was the one parent who brought paper towels, baby wipes, and lots of water and Gatorade. It came in handy. Unfortunately, my daughter was one of the victims. While she will never forget how car sick she got on this trip, she has a much fonder and stronger memory from that day because of a plan I hatched immediately after finding out I was selected as a parent chaperone.

The plot required a rock. Not just any rock. A rock of a certain size, not too big, not too small, but just the right size. It had to be impressive but believable. The rock also needed to have some specific features. Not too jagged but not perfectly smooth, either. The winning rock was about two inches in length, about an inch around, and about an inch wide.

The other part of the plot required a can of gold spray paint. For one week leading up to the field trip, I would apply a coat or two of gold paint to my "just right" rock to make it look like a gold nugget. My daughter was also involved in the plot and oversaw quality control to make sure it was convincing enough for her classmates.

Now, for the details of the plot: I would keep the rock in my jacket pocket while all the kids were focused on panning for gold in the trough in front of them. While they were all fully engaged in this activity, I would slip the rock out of my pocket and into her gold pan. We would then start screaming and yelling in excitement to draw everyone's attention, and then raise the gold nugget in victory!

Now, back to the field trip. My poor daughter and a few other kids arrived feeling horrible. We got them all off the bus, gave them water or Gatorade, and got them moving around to get the blood flowing. As we started heading down toward the gold panning area, my daughter started to feel much better in anticipation of our plan.

The gold panning area was comprised of a long trough with dirt, sand, water, and hopefully some gold nuggets or dust. On one side of the trough were some bleachers, and there were several park rangers and staffers around to demonstrate and help the students with their gold panning technique. We took our seats on the bleachers while another group was at the trough, panning away. The park ranger started talking to us about the history of Columbia, the Gold Rush, and how to pan for gold. Once the other group was finished, the park ranger invited us down to the trough, so we grabbed our gold pans and took our places.

After everyone had settled in and started swirling away with their gold pans, I asked my daughter if she was ready to execute our plot. She smiled wide and nodded. I secretly took the "gold" nugget from my pocket and dropped it into her pan. I yelled, "What's that?" and we started screaming and yelling in excitement. Everyone stopped what they were doing and turned toward us, including the park ranger who was giving his presentation to the next group seated on the bleachers behind us. I held the "gold" nugget up as high as possible to show everyone. I took a look at the parents and kids to the left and right of me, jaws agape with astonishment. I held it for a few seconds and then told everyone, "It's fake." My daughter and I laughed first, then the rest of the kids started to laugh, and the park ranger behind us carried on with his presentation as if nothing happened.

The ride home was much more enjoyable. My daughter felt better having pulled off a great prank, and I felt good because we gave all those kids and parents a memory beyond just going on a field trip. Kids and parents came up to us on the long bus ride home and asked to see the "gold" nugget up close. Without fail, each boy and girl would smile and laugh as they inspected it.

The next day, at school drop off, the father of one of the boys who went on the field trip came up to me laughing. His son had told him about the prank. He thought it was great, but his son was apparently a little mad at me for doing it. He told me that he asked his son, "Think about it. It's pretty funny right?" His son agreed. I hope that every one of the kids will remember this prank and carry it on when their fourth graders head up to California Gold Country.

As a final note, fourth grade would be the last year my daughter would attend that school. On her last day, we decided to give her teacher, Ms. Jaramillo, something very important as part of her teacher's gift. Ms. Jaramillo has the "gold," and hopefully she's had a lot of fun with it on her other fourth grade field trips. (I must admit though, I kind of wish we had kept it!)

"So long as the memory of certain beloved friends
lives in my heart, I shall say that life is good."

— Helen Keller

"Your smile is your logo. Your personality is your business
card. How you leave others feeling after an experience
with you becomes your trademark."

— Jay Danzie

TOM-ISM: "Real wealth is comprised of priceless memories."

LOOK UP! What memories can you make with family, friends, and loved ones?

LOOK AROUND! How can you make each day more memorable by mining priceless memories for those in your life?

LOOK AHEAD! What seeds are you planting for your children to make memories with their kids and grandkids?

CHAPTER 23

BLESSED BY AN ELEPHANT

"Remember that God will answer your prayers in His own timing and in ways you might not expect."

—Tony Dungy

"'You cannot leave Africa,' Africa said, 'It is always with you, there inside your head. Our rivers run in currents in the swirl of your thumbprints, our drumbeats counting out your pulse, our coastline the silhouette of your soul.'"

—Bridget Dore, South African Poet

I often say that God answers your prayers, but you need to listen with your soul, not your ears. Let me tell you about a story from many years ago when a prayer of mine was answered… by an elephant.

I am an animal lover, and elephants have always been my favorite. I can't remember the exact reason why, but I think it has to do with the fact that they always seem to be smiling. I had seen elephants in zoos and always wanted to see them in the wild, but I never saved up the money or made the time available to do that.

In 2016, I was still working my way back financially from the aftermath of a divorce. I was working in sales and things were going well, but with the added expenses of alimony and child support, money was tight. My dream trip to Africa was on the horizon once alimony and child support were no longer required. My boss sat me down one day and said, "I'm tired of hearing you talk about Africa 'someday.' Your bonus is an airline ticket to Nairobi, but you must use it in six months, or it goes away."

He left me no choice but to go! And I'm glad I did.

I contacted my friends from Save The Elephants, based in Kenya, and they helped me make the travel arrangements to stay at their Elephant Watch Camp in the Samburu region of Kenya. I also contacted the David Sheldrick Trust Orphanage where I fostered several baby elephants that were orphaned after their mothers were poached for the illegal ivory trade. The elephant orphanage is located near Nairobi, and I decided to visit it twice during my trip.

I arrived in Nairobi, and it took two hours to get through customs. In Nairobi, when it is break time, it is break time. People will leave their positions and close things down. I stood in a crowded room waiting for customs people to return to their desks. In the meantime, I had given my luggage ticket to a driver who met me with a sign bearing my name, his services were arranged by my friends at Save The Elephants. For all I knew, he was currently selling everything in my luggage on the local version of eBay. Luckily, he wasn't.

I got through customs, met my driver, and headed to my hotel for the night near Wilson Airfield, where I would be departing from early the next day to Buffalo Springs airport in the Samburu region. The first wild animals I saw were the three mosquitos in my hotel room. Mosquitos carry malaria, and even though I had shots to prevent it, malaria was not something I wanted to catch.

The next morning, I checked out of my room and headed to the café at the hotel. The hotel and café had been there for many years. The café had many photographs, airplane parts, and paintings on the wall to celebrate the history of Kenya, both the native history and the European Colonialist version. As someone who studies history, I often find myself wondering what it was like to live there during those times.

I got on my flight, which was a twin-engine Otter aircraft offering little room for someone who is 6 feet 3 inches tall and 200 pounds. The runway would be the last patch of asphalt I would see for the next week. After three stops at other airports with dirt or gravel runways, we arrived at Buffalo Springs airstrip. Out of the window, I could see two Samburu warriors dressed in their native garb, waiting for me by a Jeep. I was able to extricate myself from the aircraft and breathed in the fresh air of the African bush for the first time.

Time to search for elephants! My Samburu warrior guides packed my luggage in the Jeep, and off we went.

In Kenya, one of the predominant languages is Swahili, so I learned the Swahili word for every animal we encountered. In Swahili, there are two words for elephant: "Tembo" (tehm bow) and "Ndovu" (n doh voo). The first wild animal I saw after landing in the Samburu region was a secretary bird. I never saw any mosquitos while in the bush, but I did get stung by a large insect and hoped it wasn't venomous or had planted eggs under my skin. I hoped I wouldn't recreate that famous scene from the movie *Alien* in a few weeks.

As we drove, the next animals I saw were a small group of zebras. A group of zebras is called a "dazzle." What a great name! They were dazzling. They can also be called a "herd" or a "zeal." The Swahili word for zebra is "pundamilia" which translates to "striped donkey." As we continued driving, we got closer to the river. The Ewaso Ngiro river runs through the part of Kenya near the Elephant Watch Camp where I would be staying. I noticed my guides sticking their heads out looking down towards the road and pointing. I asked them what they were doing, and they replied, "Lion tracks, and they're fresh. They've just been here. But there are elephants over there, so we will come back." We headed off toward the river to find elephants.

We headed down the dirt road toward the river and my guides started pointing ahead as they turned the Jeep for a better view. "Elephants!" A small group were lined up in the river, drinking and tossing water on their backs through their trunks. A group of elephants is usually called a herd, but sometimes you will hear a group of elephants being called a "memory" or a "parade." It was quite a memory for me! It was both great and humbling to see them on their own terms, in their own environment, where I was a small part of their landscape.

I never felt at risk among them, even when they would move in close to the Jeep and actually reach in with their trunks to sniff me or walk from one side of the Jeep to the other as I slid back and forth to get better pictures. You will often hear me say that most people only experience animals on Man's terms at zoos or animal parks, but to fully appreciate an animal, Man needs to go meet them in the wild on the Animals' terms. Experiencing these amazing creatures on their terms was indeed incredible. While I never felt in danger, I was in awe of their power and the fact that at any time of their choosing, they could flip the Jeep over or pull me out of it with their trunks. It was a humbling experience, but I felt blessed to be able to co-exist with them and bond with them in the wild as an animal lover. We did go back and find the two lionesses whose tracks we saw earlier. They were magnificent and awe-inspiring as well! Little did I know that these first experiences with these elephants (and lions) would lead to an even more amazing experience with one big bull elephant.

During one of my safaris in the national park surrounding the Elephant Watch Camp, we came across another, larger herd of elephants. As we were parked on the dirt road with elephants feeding all around our Jeep, a large bull elephant, standing about twelve feet high at his head, slowly made his way toward us. Watching him approach reminded me of the special effects dinosaurs in the *Jurassic Park* movies. This was the largest elephant I saw on the trip, and he kept coming toward us. He decided to stop right next to me, facing me. He was about twelve feet high and huge! He was within three feet of the Jeep. He was rumbling, flapping his ears, and shaking his head at me! There's that party game question of "What's one super-power do you wish you had?" Mine would have to be the ability to talk to animals, and it would have come in handy right then! The guide driving the Jeep said, "Don't be afraid." I replied, "Are you kidding? This is awesome!" And it was. I sat still and just looked at him. After a while, I guess he decided I was okay, and he made his way down the road.

The Save The Elephants team names both elephant herds and individual animals. For example, one of the herds is called "The Royals," and they have names of royal family members of England. Another group is "The Artists," and they are named after famous international artists. So, I had to ask my guide, "What was his name?" "Lemaiyan," he replied. "What does that mean in English?" I asked. And he replied, "Blessing." I got chills and broke down a bit. I had to fly halfway around the world to get to a point in the middle of nowhere in the Kenyan bush at a particular time to have an enormous bull elephant named "Blessing" visit me. This was not a random event, but a prayer answered. And since I am an animal lover whose favorite animal is an elephant, who chose St. Francis of Assisi, the Patron Saint of Animals, as his confirmation name —why wouldn't God send me an elephant to bless me and answer my prayers? No words were spoken, but the feelings of that experience consumed me and will live with me forever.

There is an African Proverb that says, "When elephants fight, it is the grass that suffers."

After having that up close experience with Lamaiyan, I have pity on any African grass, or other vegetation and animals, that may be nearby when two elephant bulls fight.

As I mentioned earlier, seeing animals in a zoo is much different than seeing them in their natural habitat. In the wild, you see the animals on their terms, not Man's, and it is a very different and humbling experience.

"When I started counting my blessings,
my whole life turned around."

— Willie Nelson

"LIFE, is good when you are happy.
But life is better when other people are
happy because of you.
People may not reward you, or thank you for what you do,
But when God is your reason for loving and giving,
You will receive a greater blessing in return."

— Khalil Gibran

TOM-ISM: "God answers our prayers, but we need to listen with our souls."

LOOK UP! Keep an open heart and mind, and be forever watchful. You never know when or in what uniquely personal way your prayers will be answered.

LOOK AROUND! Do not act like prey. There might be a lion right behind you!

LOOK AHEAD! What is a childhood dream of yours that you need to make plans to experience?

CHAPTER 24

UNDERSTANDING

"To love without knowing how to love wounds the person we love. To know how to love someone, we have to understand them. To understand, we need to listen."

—Thich Nhat Hanh

We never know what other people may be going through. We never know what internal challenges someone may be facing in their life. This is why it is so important to show everyone empathy and understanding in all situations. Am I good at this? I like to think so, but I'm sure I could use a little help and improvement, especially while driving in L.A. traffic!

Why is understanding important?

Understanding leads to identifying common ground.

Understanding leads to greater knowledge of the other person and the world around us.

Understanding leads to empathy.

Understanding leads to forgiveness.

Understanding leads to peace.

Understanding leads to love.

The fastest path to understanding is creating an open and trusted channel of communication. This involves a caring, active listener who is not in a hurry to answer but is listening to understand.

A good friend of mine named Cornell who lives in the Chicago area told me a great line that either his mother or grandmother shared with him: "It is hard to hate someone from up close." This line stuck with me because it is so true. Getting to know someone on their territory, or up close, is the root of understanding. If we all took this approach, how much better could the world be?

We cannot fully appreciate or understand another's perspective or experience from a distance. We must engage to understand, and the closer the engagement, the better. The best way to do this is face to face . Engage in an open discussion with no judgement. Approach things with an open heart and an open mind. Actively listen. Agree with each other, or agree to disagree, but always depart as friends.

There is a lot of hate, or perceived hate, out there. A lot of this hate results from people not engaging up close and having open, and intellectually honest conversations. We need to meet each other with open hearts, open minds, and a little grace.

Understanding doesn't always mean agreement. We can understand and disagree. We can disagree, still love each other, and maintain family ties and friendships.

LOOK UP! Who can you get closer with to better understand them?

LOOK AROUND! Engage, listen, understand, discuss, and always part as friends.

LOOK AHEAD! We build a better collective future by listening and being open minded.

CHAPTER 25

PERSONAL PEACE

"If you cannot find peace within yourself, you will never find it anywhere else."

—Marvin Gaye

"Don't hope that events will turn out the way you want, welcome events in whichever way they happen, this is the path to peace."

—Epictetus

I started the year stating that my guide word for this year was "peace." Personal peace. We can be at war with ourselves by overthinking and stressing out over outside factors, so personal peace is an amazing thing to focus on and will likely be one of my words for every year going forward.

Personal peace is a recognition that I can set my own goals, draw my own boundaries, and not let the outside world control my world so much. Obviously, I need to interact with other people every day, work with people every day, and share the roads with people every day, so I don't have total control over the outside variables that impact my peace, but I do have the ability to control how I respond to these external variables, which is the key to my inner peace.

The things that I focus on to achieve greater personal peace are the following:

1. My relationship with God.

2. My relationships with family and friends.

3. My Trees of Joy.

4. My Anchors of Hope.

5. Setting personal goals and boundaries.

6. Setting realistic goals and expectations.

7. Identifying my purpose and taking action toward it.

8. Minimizing chaos in my life.

9. Exercise and personal health.

As you grow older, your priorities shift. How, where, and with whom you expend your energy begins to change. What you are willing to put up with begins to change, and you adjust your life accordingly to better serve your purpose and your dreams. You start to live your life with a different attitude, different boundaries, and a different definition of success. You start to measure your life on your own parameters rather than society's parameters. You understand that the clock is ticking, and therefore, you need to be less selfless with your time and energy.

Shaquille O'Neal once said, "The older you get, the more you realize how precious life is. You have no desire for drama, conflict, or stress. You just want good friends, a cozy home, food on the table, and people who make you happy." Your focus changes to living each day with more presence and intention rather than focusing on mistakes of the past, or days in the future that you may never see. Dr. Wayne Dyer said that "Peace is the result of retraining your mind to process life as it is, rather than as you think it should be." We can negatively impact our personal peace when we set unrealistic goals and expectations for ourselves or focus only on one specific outcome to define our happiness.

A very popular phrase we all hear is, "It is what it is." But I would rather live by the following:

TOM-ISM: "It is what you make of it."

This approach gives you some say in how you respond to "what is," versus throwing your hands up and taking no action that benefits you.

"Do not let the behavior of others destroy your inner peace."

— Dalai Lama

"If you are depressed, you are living in the past. If you are anxious, you are living in the future. If you are at peace, you are living in the present."

— Lao Tzu

LOOK UP! How can you simplify your life and add to your personal peace?

LOOK AROUND! Do you really need everything in your life, or can you live without certain things and declutter, both materially and spiritually?

LOOK AHEAD! What dreams do you still have, and what steps can you take today to move closer to them?

KEEP GOING! Don't give up on your dreams! Life is too short!

CHAPTER 26

HUMBLE YOURSELF

"The gate of heaven is very low; only the humble can enter it."

— St. Elizabeth Ann Seton

"Being humble means recognizing that we are not on earth to see how important we can become, but to see how much difference we can make in the lives of others."

— Gordon B. Hinckley

Everyone should seek to be humbled to better understand themselves, the world, and our universe. Society seems to be more and more focused on ego, self-importance, competition, "crushing it," one-upmanship, trolling, "scoreboard," and selfies. It is important for the species of Man to be humbled. We are a tremendous species capable of greatness and kindness but also of great evil. Just look around the world at all the global conflicts fueled by evil and greed. While I don't celebrate natural disasters and human suffering, nature tends to find ways to remind us of our smallness from time to time. Man might be able to be manage or leverage nature, but Man can never conquer nature. Nature will always have the last word. Nature always has "scoreboard."

Some examples of things in nature that have humbled me:

- → Elephants in Africa
- → Redwood trees (and other trees)

- → Oceans
- → Planets
- → Stars
- → Mountains
- → Lions in Africa
- → Weather
- → Earthquakes
- → Whales
- → Lightning
- → Volcanoes
- → Disease
- → Our Solar System
- → The Universe

It is important to feel small sometimes. It is important to gain from humility. When I was in the Samburu region in Africa, in the middle of nowhere in Kenya, I had such a perspective. Without local guides who knew the region, I was as good as dead. Without weapons, Man isn't so tough. Without weapons, Man stands no chance against elephants, lions, hippos, rhinos, crocodiles, painted dogs, hyenas, leopards, and various venomous snakes. But there is power in humility. There is power in meeting a bull elephant or a lioness, face to face , on their terms, not Mans'. There is a power in co-existence. There is a lot of talk about Man destroying the earth through nuclear war, climate change, or various other means. How ego-centric of us! Man cannot destroy the world. Man can only destroy himself. Man might be able to destroy other life on Earth as well, but nature will always find a way to survive and continue forward. Nature will find a way. Nature has "scoreboard."

"Strive for humility, because totalitarian pride manifests itself in intolerance, oppression, torture and death."

— Jordan Petersen

"Self-praise is for losers. Be a winner. Stand for something. Always have class and be humble."

— John Madden

LOOK UP! Notice the beauty and power of nature!

LOOK AROUND! What makes you feel small? What humbles you?

LOOK AHEAD! Co-exist with nature and take care of the Earth!

KEEP GOING! Earth will keep going, but the species of Man will not if we don't get our act together and take care of each other and our planet.

CHAPTER 27

GLASSES AND DOORS

"If you see your glass as half empty, then pour it into a smaller glass and stop bitching."

—Unknown

"Old ways won't open new doors."

—Unknown

"Not knowing when the Dawn will come, I open every Door."

—from "Not knowing when the Dawn will come"
by Emily Dickenson, 1619

THE GLASS

It's an age-old question: Is the glass half empty or half full? There are others who argue that what's missing is the notion that the glass is refillable. Still others argue that you should feel fortunate to even have a glass, because some people don't, and be greatful that there is something in the glass. All of these are relevant points of view.

Be happy that you have access to clean water.

Be happy that you can refill it at any time.

Why are you focused on a glass when there is a life to live, and time is ticking away?

THE DOOR

What's on the other side of the door?

Fear

Love

Pain

Success

Failure

Opportunity

What is always on the other side of a door is a new experience, whether good or bad. You can't experience new things without finding and opening new doors. New doors to houses, class-rooms, restaurants, airplanes, hotels, businesses, and many other doors that will offer us an opportunity to learn and evolve.

When a door is presented to you, knock on it and see if some-one answers. If the door opens, look inside and see if it is worth staying. If not, find a new door.

LOOK UP! You can't see opportunities if your head is looking down at your phone!

LOOK AROUND! What doors do you see that you can knock on or take a look inside?

LOOK AHEAD! What doors would you like to enter, and what preparation is required to become qualified to enter them?

KEEP GOING! New doors will present themselves to you.

CHAPTER 28

KINDNESS

"Sometimes it takes only one act of kindness and
caring to change a person's life."

— Jackie Chan

"Carry out a random act of kindness, with no expectation of
reward, safe in the knowledge that one day
someone might do the same for you."

—Princess Diana

Years ago, I would say to people, "The day is coming soon where we will be forced to take care of each other in ways we could never imagine." This was years before Covid-19 hit, but it was certainly one of the events I was predicting. While there were several examples of good people doing wonderful things to help others, there were also the examples of people hoarding toilet paper and rioting during 2020 and into early 2021 that made me shake my head. What was more maddening is that people used these riots to further divide the country. They didn't care about unifying us because unifying us would limit their political power and their narrative. It disgusted me. I am still convinced that more days are coming when we will need to take care of each other, and I hope we do a better job of it next time. The world seems to be on fire, and there are plenty of people in positions of leadership who pour fuel on the fire while they claim to be using a fire extinguisher.

How can we best take care of each other? Let's start by treating people with a little more kindness. Kindness is something that we could all use more of and share more of, but it tends to be an afterthought in our "hustle and bustle, I've got to get mine, I need to crush it today" world.

It is said that "hurt people, hurt people." It is personal hurt that tends to block our kindness toward others. But it doesn't take much to be a kind person who is kind toward others. It is a mindset. It is an attitude. It is a lifestyle that says no matter what negativity is thrown my way, I won't engage in it. I will offer kindness. Kindness is easy. It is a smile to a stranger, it is holding a door open for someone, it is letting a person merge in front of you in traffic, it is offering some of your precious time to others when they need help. I also believe that acting with kindness can start a domino effect. Your act of kindness toward another person might be the positive energy that they need to do an act of kindness themselves, and so on, and so on.

Try to do one kind thing for someone each day and watch how it multiplies.

"Be good to people. You will be remembered more
for kindness than any level of success
you could possibly attain."
— Mandy Hale

"If you try to be kind to people, you'll be on the
road to a good life."
— George Dunn, WWII Veteran

It seems like there is a lot of division in our country and in the world. Countries and peoples are at war or on the brink of war. Politicians focus on division rather than unity, and many in the media do the same. We must recognize what they are doing and reject it! We were not put on Earth to destroy each other, but to lift each other up. We are here to pursue our purpose and our dreams and to help those we love and others we meet to move forward toward their purposes and dreams. Those who wish to put a wedge between us or pull us further apart are engaging in evil behavior. We should be able to associate with people whose company we enjoy regardless of our differences, and especially regardless of political party affiliation.

Ellen DeGeneres said it best: "The fact is that I am friends with a lot of people who don't share the same beliefs that I have. We are all different, and I think we've forgotten that that's OK that we are all different...But just because I don't agree with someone on everything doesn't mean that I am not going to be friends with them. When I say be kind to one another, I don't mean only the people that think the same way you do. I mean be kind to everyone."

We should all embrace this attitude to make our world a better place. "Be kind to everyone." What a novel concept! Not hard to do if you make it a priority (okay, a little harder to do when driving in traffic, but we can try our best nonetheless).

You probably have heard someone say, "Be kind to everyone because you have no idea what they are going through." I think this is a great way to start each day. Think of the times when you needed a little more kindness and grace. Start each day being kinder to yourself, and then let that kindness flow outward to others. What if we all started our days with the intention of being kind? How would the world look?

As Fred Rogers from the television show *Mr. Roger's Neighborhood* said, "Imagine what our real neighborhoods would be like if each of us offered, as a matter of course, just one kind word to another person." Think about it: What motivates you more in your daily life, someone who offers a polite request or someone who demands that you do something?

We can be captains of industry, business leaders, police officers, or teachers and still be kind. We can achieve great things while being kind. We can change hearts and minds by being kind. As posited by philosopher Jean Jacques Rousseau, "What wisdom can you find that is greater than kindness?" We can expand this wisdom of kindness further through an American proverb: "Kindness is the noblest weapon with which to conquer." Kindness is an attitude or mindset that starts in each of our hearts and minds as we get out of bed each day. If we start our days with the intention of being kind, it will change our world in a positive way, even if others decide not to join in. Be kind regardless.

Our kindness can lift people up. Think of how easy it is to change someone's day just by smiling at them. How does it change your day or attitude if they smile back?

IMPACT:

"You never really know the true impact you have
on those around you.
You never know how much someone needed that
smile you gave them.
You never know how much your kindness turned
someone's entire life around.
You never know how much someone needed that
long hug or deep talk.
So don't wait to be kind.
Don't wait for someone else to be kind first.
Don't wait for better circumstances or for
someone to change.
Just be kind, because you never know how much
someone needs it."

— Nikki Banas

"Kindness is more important than deeds.
It is an attitude,
An expression,
A look,
A touch.
It is anything that lifts another person."

— Plato

"Three things in human life are important. The first is to be
kind. The second is to be kind. And the third is to be kind."

— Henry James

LOOK UP! Share a smile with someone!

LOOK AROUND AND LOOK AHEAD! Where can you inject some kindness to improve the situation?

KEEP GOING! Continue to be kind even if others are not!

LOOK AHEAD! WHAT KIND OF LIFE DO YOU WANT?

CHAPTER 29

PARENTING
(WINNING THE PARENT LOTTERY)

"If you want to change the world, go
home and love your family."

—Mother Teresa

"Having one child makes you a parent,
having two makes you a referee."

—David Frost, British TV host

Like it or not, our parents are the reason we are here. Our parents are the people who shape our world from day one. They are our caretakers, our teachers, our guardians, and hopefully, our friends as we enter adulthood. Parenting is the most important job out there.

For some, parental relationships are challenging. Parents can be mentally or physically abusive. They can suffer from addiction. They can divorce, create division, and alienate affection. Parents are not perfect, but hopefully, they are responsible and love and support their children as best they can.

While I didn't realize it until I got older, I won the parent lottery. They say that comparison is the thief of joy. While that can be true, comparison of my parents with other parents I have come across throughout my life has been a source of joy...and great relief.

While you are growing up and your parents are setting the rules, you may view them as tyrants, but they are really trying to protect you. I was lucky that my parents cared. They wanted us to succeed. They reinforced the importance of God, education, pursuing excellence, having manners, and treating everyone with respect.

I was lucky that my parents stayed together. They had their share of fights and arguments, but they fought harder for their marriage than they did with each other. They found solutions. They stayed together and provided a stable and loving environment for their kids to grow up. I was not successful in staying married, and I see the negative impact of that on my kids.

The other reasons that I say that I won the parent lottery are:

- → They were sober.
- → They cared about our education, our futures, and our success.
- → They provided our basic needs (food, clothing, shelter, health, and safety).
- → They loved us (sometimes tough love, but love nonetheless).
- → They emphasized special days in our lives, like holidays and birthdays, and made them special.
- → They taught us to love our country.
- → They gave us a foundation of faith in God.
- → They tried to make every day a gift.

BECOMING A PARENT

You will understand your parents better the moment you become one. It all starts to make sense. All the things that your parents did that you disagreed with or didn't understand will become clearer. You may still disagree, but you will have a deeper understanding of why they did what they did.

I remember my brother once complaining to me that mom and dad worried about him too much, and they should stop because he is an adult. My brother did not have kids of his own, so I offered the following: "It doesn't matter if they're in their nineties and you are in your seventies, you are still their son, and they will always worry about you." Worry is baked into parenthood.

Becoming a parent is the greatest thing that ever happened to me. I always ask new parents if they can describe the experience in one word. They all struggle with an answer. The best word I have come up with is "magical." The range of emotions you feel, from overwhelming love, to fear, to a drive to provide, to utter joy — magical is as close as I can come, and it still doesn't do it justice.

I take the job and responsibility of parenting very seriously. Children are human beings that need to be protected, educated, and coached as they grow up. They are not accessories for your life. I remember being in a job interview once where the hiring manager asked me the following hypothetical: "It's your daughter's birthday, and you are asked to go to China to finalize a big deal. What would you do?" At the time, my daughter was seven, so the answer was easy. I replied, "I ask the client to move the date, and I celebrate my daughter's birthday. If I do my job right, I schedule around that date, and if the client is worth having, they will understand." I didn't get the job, but I do wonder how many important family dates and events this hiring manager missed over his career.

I feel a little sorry for the oldest child in any new family. New parents are freaks. We don't know what we're doing. We are overprotective. Every sniffle is a reason to call a doctor or dial 911.

Whenever I meet new parents, I give them a few pieces of advice (which I guess we can officially call Tom-isms at this point):

1. The best gift you can give your children is a happy, strong marriage or relationship with the other parent. Keep dating your spouse or the other parent!

2. Children don't come with an owner's manual; that's why there are grandparents! Don't be too proud to seek their advice and get them involved (especially to help with the kids so you can follow through on that date-your-spouse advice)!

Before you know it, these little ones will become college graduates. It is important to enjoy every stage in their growth and development. I once read somewhere that "becoming a parent is the one job where success is measured by your ability to teach the ones you love the most how to live without you." Tough job description! But parenting is tough every day. It is hard work, but it is a fulfilling purpose. I love the quote from Neil Postman, "Children are the living messages we send to a time we will not see."

←—The best picture I ever took! Me with my son and daughter at Disneyland. They were both tired and wanted to be carried. This is the result.

←—We re-created the photo in subsequent years. When the kids hit their teenage and young adult years and it became less interesting to them. I hope to take more of these in the future, with either them or me carrying their children, my grandkids!

"If you think their messy room is hard to look at,
just wait until it's empty."

— Unknown

"I want you to think about your parents
for a moment.
Your birthday is their celebration.
Your happiness is their joy.
Your future is their legacy.
If they had to bury you, it would kill them.
So please, next time they say, 'be safe', or 'let me
know when you get there ok',
Don't just brush it off.
Because to them, you are everything."

— Unknown

TOM-ISM: "Every professional title that I ever attain will always report to my title of 'Dad.'"

LOOK UP! When was the last time you spoke to your parents or to your kids? Call them! Meet with them!

LOOK AROUND: Take advantage of the time you have together.

LOOK AHEAD: Create memories now! They grow up so fast!!!

CHAPTER 30

BE A "COG"

"You are a Child of God. You are wonderfully made.
Dearly loved. And precious in His sight."

—Based on Psalm 139

"Do not be dismayed by the brokenness of the world. All
things break. And all things can be mended. Not with time,
as they say, but with intention. So, go! Love intentionally,
extravagantly, unconditionally. The broken world
waits in darkness for the light that is you."

—L.R. Knost, Award Winning Author

"No matter what they do, every person on earth plays a
central role in the history of the world.
And normally, they don't know it."

—Paul Coelho, *The Alchemist*

I am amazed at what is going on in the world. The hate. The killing. I thought we had evolved beyond that, having experienced two world wars in the last hundred plus years and several other global conflicts. But the unfortunate truth is that peace is not the normal state for mankind.

In my mind, we should all be good "COGs." And also in my mind, "COG" should not stand for "Creature Of Government" or "Chaos Over Good." It does not stand for "Cost of Goods" or "Creepy Office Guy," which my sister recently clued me in on.

Aside from the above definitions, what comes to mind when you hear the word "COG?" What exactly is a "cog?" Oxford Languages defines "cog" as the following:

"NOUN: a wheel or bar with a series of projections on its edge, which transfers motion by engaging with projections on another wheel or bar."

A cog is a gear or a moving part of a machine or system.

The word cog can also be used to define a minor player in an organization.

But my definition of "COG" is something much bigger and far more important. Whether looking at things from a nation-to-nation perspective or from one political party to the other, I believe there is more that unites us than divides us. This is where I came up my concept and definition of "COG."

To me, "COG" stands for "Child Of God."

When I apply that definition, no one is a "minor player."

I use this specific definition because it unifies us at a very fundamental level:

As members of the Universe.

As members of a universal family.

As brothers and sisters as a base relationship.

TOM-ISM: "We are all put on this Earth to serve a purpose, and I don't believe it is to destroy each other."

We are all COGs in the machine of the Earth and the Universe, but we allow man-made, societal definitions, politics, and social media affect how we define ourselves and our purpose.

We allow political parties to distract us from what makes us good, productive, thoughtful, and caring COGs in this world, which means that we are not uniting by what we have in common.

And these man-made distractions are delivered to us how? Mostly through screens! That is why it is important to look up from these screens, put them down, and spend more quality time with family, friends, nature, and our communities.

When COGs are not united and working in their purpose, the entire machine's performance is negatively affected.

We are all COGs in the complex machine of nature. When we are all productive COGs in nature's machine, the world runs smoothly. We take care of each other, we love each other, and we live in peace.

COG in my book also stands for "Citizen of Good."

COG, in my book, can also mean "Creator of Grace."

I am sure there are other positive descriptions that can make this acronym, and I'm sure if this idea catches on, there will be several other suggestions, both positive and negative.

So, take your pick of a positive definition of COG and become one. An active one. One that starts a positive change in the world.

When we look up from our screens, look around, and look even higher, we can identify ways to become better Children of God, better Citizens of Good, and better Creators of Grace. It is a mindset and a mission that we can take littles steps toward every minute of every day. It starts in our own hearts, and when it changes our behaviors, the rest of the world will take notice of the increased intensity of our light and possibly change as well. Maybe they will put down their man-made arms of destruction to reach out with the arms they have been given, and embrace their fellow humans.

"Do your little bit of good where you are, it is those little bits of good put all together that overwhelm the world."

— Desmond Tutu

A REAL LIFE "COG"

There is a big cat rescue operation in Southern California called Shambala Reserve. It was founded, and is still owned, by the actress Tippi Hedren. Ms. Hedren is probably best known for her role in the classic Alfred Hitchcock film *The Birds*.

I used to sponsor a mountain lion named Trinity. When Trinity passed away, the folks at Shambala invited me to come to their next event to pick out a new cat to "adopt." Since I supported a mountain lion previously, I wanted to sponsor another mountain lion at the reserve. They had several new cats that had come in as rescues from roadside zoos or had lost their mothers and were rescued by humans. None of their cats can be "rewilded."

As we came to an enclosure with three mountain lions, one male and two females, I watched the one mountain lion with the most attitude. When I asked his name, the reply was Cog. I nodded, smiled, and said, "That's the one." Now, I sponsor Cog with a monthly donation.

It shouldn't be too difficult to embrace this notion of COG. It starts with each of us. It is the determination and commitment to do what is right and good over what is expedient or selfish.

LOOK UP! LOOK AROUND! LOOK AHEAD! Be a COG now and into the future!

CHAPTER 31

BLINDERS

"The nature of humanity, its essence, is to feel another's pain
as one's own, and to act to take that pain away.
There is nobility in compassion, a beauty in
empathy, a grace in forgiveness."

—John Connolly

"If you want others to be happy, practice compassion.
If you want to be happy, practice compassion."

—Dalai Lama

Blinders are put on racehorses to keep them focused on the path forward and not on distractions in their periphery. In life, we can wear hypothetical blinders. They can be positive or negative. They are a positive when they keep us focused and moving forward. They are negative when we use them to turn inward and focus on what is wrong with us or our current circumstances. They are also a negative when they cause us not to see the circumstances and challenges of those around us.

Blinders are what we put on metaphorically when we want to focus on something or want to deny that something has occurred. Many of us wear blinders of pain when it feels like the entire world is crushing down upon us with no escape. It seems that all we have are problems, that the world is against us, and that we cannot do anything right. At such times, it is good to have a dose of perspective, and usually it comes with what I call a "divine slap" across the face. What is a divine slap? It is a message from God and the universe that yes, your problems are yours, and you must carry them and solve them as best you can. But it is also the recognition that someone, somewhere has it worse off, and they are somehow dealing with it.

I have received that divine slap many times. If we open our minds and think deeply about it, I think we all have. The divine slap gives us perspective. The divine slap gives us empathy. The divine slap causes us to take our own blinders off so that we can grow.

Everybody has their stuff to carry. Sometimes we need people to carry it for us for a while until we can regain our strength and continue to bear the weight or find a better way to carry it. Thank God for friends who help! But there are some things that only God can carry, and this is where the dose of perspective hits home.

I was recently lamenting the fact that I had to deal with some unexpected home repairs. Why did this need to happen now? How am I going to pay for it? At the same time, I was contemplating this, I got news that the daughter of an extended family member was going into emergency surgery to remove a brain tumor. Her reality jolted me back with a new perspective on the size of my problems in comparison: very small.

PERSPECTIVE AND EMPATHY

Several years ago, I was going through a divorce, trying to keep a job under heavy management scrutiny, and my son was dealing with a bad leg injury. I was mad at God, asking," Why him?" "Why me?" Angry at the world and at God for yet another major challenge to deal with, I was about to receive another divine slap. The only available bed at the hospital was in the children's cancer ward, where I watched brave little kids and teens coping and fighting with a positive energy. I also saw their parents trying to stay brave, but I felt their underlying pain. With time, my son was going to get better. With time, their children might be gone. I was trying to fast forward while everyone else in that ward was trying to slow time to a crawl.

PERSPECTIVE AND EMPATHY

I recently participated in some events where I was once again given that divine slap. I was in a group setting with some wonderful people, all of whom were carrying weight that I'm not sure I'd be qualified to carry for them . I heard stories of lost children and lost spouses, or from parents dealing with children with special needs.

Spending time hearing their stories gave me yet another dose of perspective. It also showed me there are TRUE heroes out there who are achieving victory over battles we will likely never hear about. Society tends to point us to heroes and idols that possess certain athletic or entertaining talents, but there are real heroes out there who are regular folks doing whatever is necessary, and then some, on a daily basis for the benefit of their children and families.

There is a saying that God only gives you what you can handle. I believe this is true, which made me realize how much greater their character, talents, and faith must be since I'm not sure that I could measure up to that level.

PERSPECTIVE AND EMPATHY

I am thankful for these little reminders that my blinders need to come off to fully engage with the world around me. My blinders need to come off to give me perspective, to build empathy, understanding, love, and to be more self-less.

"The world is hungry for goodness and recognizes it when it sees it…When we glimpse it in people we applaud them for it. We long to be just a little like them. Through them we let the world's pain into our hearts, and we find compassion."

— Archbishop Desmond Tutu

"Nothing is more important than empathy for another human being's suffering. Nothing. Not a career, not wealth, not intelligence, certainly not status. We have to feel for one another if we're going to survive with dignity."

— Audrey Hepburn, Actress

GIVE US THIS DAY...

When the going gets a little tough, and we have our blinders on, we often forget that each day is a gift. Each day is an opportunity to do something new, to improve ourselves, to learn new things, to meet people, etc. Instead of being caught up and focused on the bad, let's take off our blinders and live in the present moment.

Here's a bit of a challenge! When you wake up tomorrow, take a minute to thank God for another day. Then ask Him, "OK, what do you got for me today?! Bring it on! Let's do it!"

It could be good; could be bad.

It could be challenging; could be easy.

But whatever the day brings, you've got this!

LOOK UP! Take the blinders off, and **LOOK AROUND!** Everyone is fighting a battle.

LOOK AHEAD! Run your race as best you can, helping others you encounter along the way.

KEEP GOING! Life will get better! New doors will be presented for you to open.

CHAPTER 32

CONNECTING THE DOTS

"You must be willing to leave the life that you planned in order to find the one waiting for you."

— Joseph Campbell

"Don't think. It complicates things. Just feel, and if it feels like home, then follow its path."

— R.M. Drake

As a kid, I used to love dot-to-dot books. I would go through them quickly because I wanted to see what the final picture would look like. On most occasions, I could kind of make out what the picture would be without drawing the lines, but most of the time, the outcome left me surprised, or at least the details did. Oddly enough, throughout my professional life, I find myself trying to connect the dots. Sometimes I don't like the picture that's formed.

Unlike Connect the Dots books where a pre-drawn picture is to be completed, our lives are more of a blank page, and we get to decide where to put the dots or which dots to follow. Do you ever go back and connect the dots of your life to see how you got to where you are today? Do you ever wonder what life would have been like had you connected to a different dot at various stages in your life? What if I had gone to that college instead? What if I had taken that job over the other one? What if I traveled more? What if I asked her out? All these scenarios are potential dots in our lives.

Which dots and path of dots we choose to follow will lead to a different life path. It is not healthy to look back at these decisions as regrets. They are "what ifs." We must look at "what is." What is the path in front of us right now? How do we make the best decision for our lives in taking the next step forward? If one of your "what ifs" is still important to you, there is nothing stopping you from creating that path today, except for yourself. You have the power to choose. Choose wisely!

A priest once told me that God only gives us enough light to see the next step because if he showed us the whole journey, we would be overwhelmed and might never take the next step...or connect the next dot.

People can also be dots that help us outline the picture of our lives. Where we choose to put these dots in our concentric circles of relationships will provide us with the details of the final picture of our lives.

The good news is that our path is not fully mapped out. We get to choose. And when we choose, we can either look at the dots arranged in front of us or build our own dots tied to our passions, and go in that direction. It's never too late to build your own next dot!

"What if there is a path for you that is greater
than what you can envision?

What if there is a life for you that is more than
you would even know to ask for?

What if you are inherently and unknowingly limited by your
old perspectives, your outdated ideas of what is possible?

What if all the discomfort within your being is simply
trying to redirect you to a place beyond
anything you've considered before?

What if there is more than you know?

What if there are things out there so good, you don't
even know you're waiting for them?"

— Unknown

"Do not follow where the path may lead. Go instead
where there is no path and leave a trail."

— Ralph Waldo Emerson

"We keep moving forward, opening up new doors,
and new things, because we're curious…and curiosity
keeps leading us down new paths. We are
always exploring and experimenting."

— Walt Disney

LOOK UP! What are the dots that are shaping your life?

LOOK AROUND! What kind of dot are you to others?

LOOK AHEAD! What ideal picture do you want to create as you connect future dots?

KEEP GOING! Each dot leads to adventure!

CHAPTER 33

LEGACY

"Your legacy is every life you touch."

—Maya Angelou

I had a recent conversation with my Creator that went something like this:

Me: "I have time."
God: "No you don't."

Me: "That can wait. I'll get to it."
God: "No, it can't. Do it now!"

Me: "Tomorrow will be better."
God: "Tomorrow is not guaranteed, make it better today."

Me: "I don't need to go to the doctor."
God: "Your blood pressure is too high. Your blood sugar is too high. Your A1C is too high."

My arrogance was slowly killing me. My apathy was slowly killing me. My lack of purpose was slowly killing me.

I needed to make some changes, but what changes? What legacy do I want to leave when all is said and done? I had to determine what was most important to me. I had to be more disciplined in my habits to get there. I had to stop talking about what I "might do" some time, and I had to start taking action!

NOW IS THE TIME TO TAKE ACTION TOWARDS YOUR PURPOSE AND YOUR DREAMS!

LOOK UP! What kind of life do you want to live?

Take Action!

Reverse course!

Get healthy!

Get outside!

Eat right!

Exercise! Lose weight!

Time is your greatest asset!

Time to stop being the world's best kept secret!

Time to add your unique value to the world.

Time to share.

Time to teach.

Time to love.

Every sunrise is an opportunity for a new beginning, so get started!

LASTS

There will be a day when what we do here on Earth won't matter to us anymore, but what we have done will matter to everyone whose lives we've touched. They will carry our legacy into the future. My goal is to make my legacy a positive one, especially for those I love the most.

When you leave this world, your ability to actively love the people in your life goes with you. Legacy is important, but you don't need your name on a bridge or a building. Carve your name in the hearts and minds of loved ones and others so they'll remember you, talk about you, laugh because of you, cry because of you, and smile because they knew you.

They'll remember your deeds. They'll remember your smile. They'll remember your love and how it made them feel. And then, they'll tell the next generation about you, so that they too can pass your legacy on to the next person, the next generation, and beyond. Take care of your health, and KEEP GOING because you can't add to this legacy if you are not around!

"Don't cry because it's over. Smile because it happened."
— Dr. Seuss

LOVE IS YOUR LEGACY!

LOVE IS INFINITE AND EXPONENTIAL!!!

CHAPTER 34

FEAR AND COURAGE

"Having courage does not mean that we are afraid. Having courage and showing courage means we face our fears. We are able to say, 'I have fallen, but I will get up.'"

—Maya Angelou

"Everything we've ever wanted is on the other side of fear."

—George Addair

FEAR

I was climbing the ladder for the high dive at Cupertino High School in Cupertino, California. The final test for graduating from my swimming lessons as a young boy was to jump off the high dive, and swim back to the edge of the pool. Many students get to the edge of the high dive, peer over their toes at the water below, and hesitate. But what makes us hesitate? While the thought of jumping from that height was a bit scary, what I was most afraid of was falling over the side while walking from the ladder to the edge of the board. My mom expected me to hesitate, but I just went! I did it! I took the leap, landed in the water, and swam to the edge of the pool. What I decided while going up the ladder was that I was not going to stop and look over the edge. I was going to just KEEP GOING! I didn't hesitate to think it over. I just went!

I believe that the root of fear is the unknown. Once we take the leap and get on the other side of the unknown, we can conquer the fear. Once we take the leap, we are now experienced in that activity, for better or for worse. Maybe we take the leap and everything is fine, possibly even exhilarating! Maybe we take the leap and get hurt, but either way, we've overcome the fear. We've taken the leap and gained knowledge and experience for the next situation. As Marie Curie once said, "Nothing in life is to be feared, it is only to be understood. Now is the time to understand more, so that we may fear less."

There is a funny episode of the television show *The Big Bang Theory* where they discuss the concept in quantum mechanics of Schrodinger's Cat. Don't worry, I won't (aka: can't) dive into the topic of quantum mechanics, but the story is a nice illustration of the known and unknown. An oversimplified premise of the story is that if you put a cat and some poison in a steel box, and close the box for a period, the cat will either be dead or alive, but there is no way of knowing for sure until you open the box and look. Most of our fears are based on the unknown. We tend to fear uncertainty. If you ask stock traders, the worst condition is the unknown. Money can be made on good news, and money can be made on bad news, but the unknown brings the highest risk of loss.

Ralph Waldo Emerson once said, "Fear defeats more people than any other one thing in the world." To conquer our fears, we must make the unknown known. We can do that by diving in blindly, or we can gather information and evidence to make a more calculated decision.

Once you take the leap, land safely in the water, and swim safely to shore, what is the usual reaction? "That was fun!" "Let's do it again!" Be courageous! You can't have courage without first having some level of fear or encountering something unknown.

COURAGE

"Courage does not always roar. Sometimes courage is
the quiet voice at the end of the day saying,
'I will try again tomorrow.'"

—Mary Anne Radmacher

"Courage is the first virtue that makes all
other virtues possible."

—Aristotle

What is courage? Walt Disney said that courage is "The one thing it takes to accomplish something." Courage is being afraid of something but doing it anyway.

Courage is the single mom with kids who works multiple jobs to provide for her family.

Courage is the soldier who runs toward the conflict.

Courage is the first responder who does the same.

Courage is facing a life-ending illness and fighting it until the last breath.

Courage is going down a mine shaft every day to make sure that your family has food on the table and a roof overhead.

Courage is the kid who goes to school every day knowing that he or she will likely be bullied.

Courage is being there for your kids.

Courage is doing what's right when everyone else is going in a different direction.

Courage is standing on your faith.

There are many examples of daily courage taken by regular people doing their best. Courage does not have to be something bold that everyone notices or be the headline of every news story.

"Bravery is being the only one who knows you're afraid."

— Col. David Hackworth

"I learned that courage was not the absence of fear, but the triumph over it. The brave man is not he who does not feel afraid, but he who conquers that fear."

— Nelson Mandela

COMFORT VS FEAR: A DOUBLE EDGED-SWORD

There is a great quote by Michael McNulty that says, "To be courageous, you must be afraid first." The way to avoid being afraid is to seek comfort, but comfort does not lead to personal growth. Discomfort, fear, and desire for improvement lead to growth. Many people will let fear win, and they will retreat to comfort, but our best life results from us leaving comfort to confront our fears with faith. Faith in our abilities. Faith in our resilience. Faith in our God and that He will lead us, or walk with us, through it all! There is a saying that a bird on a branch is not afraid of the branch breaking because the bird trusts its ability to fly. We need to develop the same trust in our skills to overcome our fears.

"And as we let our own light shine,
We unconsciously give other people permission
to do the same.
As we're liberated from our own fear,
Our presence automatically liberates others."

— Marianne Williamson

"I have learned over the years that when one's mind is made
up, this diminishes fear, knowing what must
be done does away with fear."

— Rosa Parks

"I fear nothing for God is with me!"

— St. Joan of Arc

LOOK UP! Listen to your inner voice! Tap into your courage!

LOOK AROUND! Take the leap! Faith over fear!

LOOK AHEAD! Get over the fear, and have some fun!

And most importantly, **KEEP GOING!**

CHAPTER 35

WHEN...THEN...

"Inaction breeds doubt and fear. Action breeds confidence and courage."

—Dale Carnegie

"Action may not always bring happiness, but there is no happiness without action."

—Benjamin Disraeli

Time is our most valuable asset. We can't buy more of it. We can't make more of it. We can only prioritize what we do with it. As we move through the years, we start to reflect more on the concept of time. As you start staring your mortality in the face, you wonder what you did with all of it. But you can't "rewind," you can't "fast forward," you can only stay on "play." And while life gives us some challenges that we would like to get through quickly by hitting "fast forward," time still keeps us in the present. Time still keeps us on "play."

How many of you, like me, are challenged with the notion of "When...Then...?" How many of you have heard yourself say, "When 'X' happens, then I'll do 'Y'?"

When I get a new job, then I'll be happier.

When I meet the right person, then I'll be happier.

When I have enough money saved, then I'll take those classes.

When my kids are grown up, then I'll pursue my dreams.

On and on...

I too suffered from the When/Then Syndrome. Some of my "whens" never happened. When you have expectations about your "whens," changing life circumstances impact the "when" and your level of preparedness for executing on your "then.

SOME "WHENS" INCLUDE:

- → Time
- → Money
- → Relationships
- → Life Circumstances
- → Health
- → Age

SOME "THEN" VARIABLES

- → Educational Pursuits
- → Hobbies
- → Life dreams
- → Goals
- → Passions
- → Purpose

But WHEN you have an idea, a passion, or a defined purpose, THEN you owe it to yourself to start working on it...NOW! Not tomorrow. Not "when" you have more time later. Not "when" you have more financial resources available. NOW!

You see, the Universe cannot conspire with you to pursue your "then" unless you change the "when" to NOW and take some action toward your passion and purpose!

Taking action now does not have to be a giant leap. It can be a baby step toward your "then." Each step in the right direction is better than being stuck in the quicksand of "when." Progress builds confidence. Confidence builds competency. Competency builds greater progress. Add a little luck and some help from your universal network, and you can accelerate this cycle further.

You can change the WHEN/THEN paradigm into a positive.

When I start writing, **then** I create content.

When I donate to charity, **then** I help others.

When I eat cleaner, **then** I improve my health.

When I exercise, **then** I lose weight.

How is this approach different from the other When/Then scenario? Upon further examination, we see that in a positive When/Then paradigm, the "when" is action oriented. In the other When/Then paradigm, the "when" is passive and anticipatory. That "when" is tied to a future outcome over which we have little control. The new, positive When/Then paradigm has us taking ownership and immediate personal action in the present to create the "thens" we desire.

I recently read a passage that I'd like to share with you entitled "Later." The author is unknown, but the message is profound.

"Talk to you later.
I'll call you later.
See you later.
We'll walk later.
I'll tell you later.
We leave everything for later, but forget that
'later' does not belong to us.
Later, our loved ones are no longer with us.
Later, we don't hear from them and we don't see them.
Later, they are just memories.
Later, the day becomes night, the force becomes
helpless, the smile becomes a grimace,
and life becomes death.
'Later' becomes 'Too late.'
Do it now!"

— "Later," Author Unknown

"It won't just happen, we have to make it happen. So, hope is all about taking action to make your hope come true."

— Dr. Jane Goodall

"Any action is often better than no action... If it is a mistake, at least you learn something, in which case it's no longer a mistake. If you remain stuck, you learn nothing."

— Eckhart Tolle

We do not control time. We have no way of knowing how much time we get in this life. Those who have been told they don't have much time left will likely tell you the following: "Don't waste it on frivolous things. Maximize your time to provide fulfillment and happiness in your life and to the lives of those you love."

This is a challenge to all of you and to myself. Let's change our "whens" to "NOWS!" Instead of saying "When/Then," let's all think in terms of "Now I am going to…(fill in the action)."

Now, I am going to go to the gym.

Now, I am going to volunteer with that charity.

Now, I am going to do yardwork.

Now, I am going to ask that girl out.

Now, I am going to tell my kids I love them.

Now, I am going to hug my partner.

Now, I am going to change my life.

Have faith! Take some action! When you have faith and take some sort of action, then you make progress toward your purpose. You open the door to infinite possibilities that are aligned with who you truly are and what you are supposed to do.

WHEN you take action,… **THEN** good things will happen!

WHEN you **LOOK UP**,… **THEN** you can see infinite opportunities!

WHEN you **KEEP GOING**,… **THEN** you will achieve your goals and fulfill your purpose!

CHAPTER 36

EVOLUTION

There is a great debate between creation and evolution. I never understood why there was such an emotional argument and why people were so entrenched in it. I am all for studying where we came from and how we got here, but I never understood the argument over what is the "absolute truth."

I remember sitting in a college classroom engaging in such a debate. It was quite a tennis match of ideas and evidence being hit back and forth over the net. Some folks focused on Charles Darwin, and some focused on the work of the Leakeys. One person even brought up scientists searching for what they call the "God particle," and still others on the *Book of Genesis*. I guess I sat there silently watching this for too long. The professor called on me and said, "Tom, you've been awfully quiet. What do you think?" My response:

"I believe God creates through evolution."

You could see heads explode and hear a pin drop simultaneously. I don't remember the exact words in the following conversation, but it went something like this:

Professor: "That's interesting. Can you explain it further?"

Tom: "Well, we're all here, so something set that in motion. That's creation. We are learning and changing every day, or 'evolving,' so evolution exists as well, and evolution will continue as long as life exists. So, in my view, God is still creating through evolution."

Am I right? Who knows, but this is what I believe. Think of how far we have come as humans: we went from discovering fire to space exploration. Think of all our progress, all our inventions, all our discoveries in medicine, science, and other disciplines. That required some evolution. We are evolving every day, graduating to the next level of human development. Scientists say we only use ten percent of our brains, so who knows what else we have in store! As the years go on, we will make new discoveries and learn more about ourselves, our world, and our universe. Some would argue that not everything we do is an evolution. Some folks argue that we should unplug the Internet. There are also people, like me, that argue that we need to do a better job of managing our screen time to get back to nature and to spend more quality time with our families.

TOM-ISM: "God creates through evolution."

LOOK UP! At all of God's creations. They are pretty amazing!

LOOK AROUND! How do you see them evolving? Are you evolving?

LOOK AHEAD! Where will we evolve to next?

KEEP GOING! Isn't that what evolution is all about?

PART IV

LOOK HIGHER AND DEEPER

CHAPTER 37

LOVE (AGAIN!)

"Where there is love there is life."

—Mahatma Gandhi

"Love is the beauty of the soul."

—St. Augustine

Love is a topic that I will continue to cover over and over because love is the answer! You might ask, "To what question?" To which I will reply, "Pretty much everything." How do we bring peace to the world? Love. How do we solve world hunger? Love. How do we end gun violence? Love. How do we solve loneliness? Love. And there are plenty of other questions to which love is the answer.

Part of the *Gotta Look Up* mission is to focus on looking higher and more spiritually to provide leadership toward a better life path. Maybe discussing love more often will help put the right energy into the Universe.

How much better would our world be today if ALL world leaders would focus on growing and improving the conditions of their country for all of their citizens rather than focusing on their historical legacies and growing their family riches? To all world leaders: your citizens do not want war! Your citizens want opportunities to live in peace and to provide a nice life for their families. That is it! Why must you pursue a path of hate and destruction? Why must you impose your will rather than promote liberty and freedom? We have countless examples in our history of the insanity and suffering of war. You are weak if you bring this suffering and hardship to your people. Do better!

Here is a Tom-ism that applies to this and appeals to ALL world leaders:

"If only world leaders would realize that the greatness of their countries resides in the accomplishments of their citizens and not the conquests of their governments."

For the most part, our so-called leaders are failing in this department. So, how do we as global citizens lead from the bottom?

LOVE THY NEIGHBOR!

A great man once said this over 2,000 years ago, and we still haven't gotten it right, so we need to try harder and do better! And it starts with me. How can I love my neighbor better? Maybe by not yelling at them when they cut me off on the freeway. Maybe by donating money or food to a family in need. Maybe by dropping off toys and blankets to an animal shelter. It's not that hard to add a little more love into the Universe.

LOVE. It is a four-letter word that, if properly implemented, can change the course of human history.

Love. The world needs a big dose of it right now.

There is too much war. Too much division. Too much hate. The sad truth is some people profit or gain power from division and hate. We don't have to play that game. Take their power away! Do not let them divide you from loving, or at least seeking to understand, your neighbor!

Love is the real power. Love is the answer, not hate.

LOVE! If all nations and peoples of the world agreed today not to teach their children how to hate, we would have a much different and better world in a generation.

Love is so important, that I think it makes sense to share this passage from 1 Corinthians again:

"Love is patient.
Love is kind.
It does not envy.
It does not boast.
It is not proud.
It does not dishonor others.
It is not self-seeking.
It is not easily angered.
It keeps no record of wrongs.
Love does not delight in evil,
But rejoices with the truth.
It always protects, always trusts, always hopes, always perseveres.
Love never fails."

— 1 Corinthians 13:4-8

In music we are told that "Love is a Battlefield," "Love Hurts," and "Love is the Drug." All of these can be true, but the truest of them all is "Love is all you need."

Love is contagious.

Love is exponential.

If you go through family turmoil of any kind, you will see people retreat to their corners, go to their perspectives, and hold onto them for dear life. A priest friend of mine, Father Brendan, gave me the best piece of advice for these types of situations. He said, "Tom, do you want to be right, or do you want to be loving?" After several silent minutes thinking it over, I realized that when I'm focused on being loving, I'm usually doing what's right, not only for that situation but for my own interests as well. So, I choose to be loving. Again, I do the best I can, but I'm not perfect and still have a long way to go in the love department. That said, an awareness of trying to be loving versus trying to be right will help you evolve your behavior.

I can hear Father Brendan's voice in my head whenever I am involved in a disagreement or argument. And if you think being loving means that you get rolled over all the time, that would be an incorrect assumption.

THE POWER OF SAYING "I LOVE YOU"

If you really want to catch someone off-guard, tell them that you love them. Then, stand back and watch them freak out. Now, I don't recommend doing this to complete strangers on the street, but that's up to you. I'm talking about saying "I love you" to the people you are close to, those who are important in your life. Friends, family, and, yes, definitely spouses and significant others. People want to hear that they are loved. It makes them feel important. It shows them that they matter.

I have lost too many friends and family members too early in life. I wish they knew how important they were to me. I hope they did, even if I never got to tell them directly. It makes me wonder, what was the last interaction I had with them? Was it positive? Did they know how important they were to me? What were the last words they heard from me? That last question is the real kicker and is the reason why I do my best to remember to tell the people I care about that I love them when we part company, just in case it is the last time we get to see each other.

I --- LOVE --- YOU!

Three little words, made up of only eight letters, form a phrase that holds so much power and emotion. Use it! Let people who matter to you know that you love them while they are still here! While you are still here! It is not that hard to increase the amount of love in the world, but each of us has to summon the courage and vulnerability to say these three words. The world needs more love, and it starts in each of our hearts.

"Love is not: It will give this to you if you do this for me.
Love is: I will give this to you so that you may shine."

— Young Pueblo

"To love someone is to learn the song in their heart and sing it to them when they have forgotten it."

— Arne Garborg,
Norwegian Writer

Let's all pledge to make sure that there's not too little love in the world! Let's start looking up and putting a little more love into the world today. If each of us concentrates on being more loving a little more each day...hate doesn't stand a chance!

LOOK UP! LOOK AROUND! Who in your life needs a little love right now?

GO LOVE THEM UP!

CHAPTER 38

THE GIRL WITH THE DRAGON PLUSHIE

I want to share a personal story I call "The Girl With The Dragon Plushie." When I tell this story live and in person, I never get through it without shedding some tears. I already feel myself welling up as I write this.

In 2014, my son broke his leg very badly. He had to be taken to the hospital in an ambulance. He broke both his tibia and fibula bad enough to require surgery for a rod and screws. While this was bad, it was only the beginning. For two weeks, he suffered excruciating pain, requiring me to take him to the emergency room on several occasions between 2 and 4 AM to get treated for the pain. The doctors tried medication after medication, and I am thankful to this day that my son did not get addicted to any of those pain killers.

For weeks, I did not get any sleep while tending to him at home or driving him to the emergency room. I was not on good terms with God, and I let Him know it. I don't remember the name of the physical therapist that made me take him to the emergency room at Stanford Hospital, but I wish I had found her weeks earlier. The medical team at Stanford diagnosed that the screws used to keep the rod in place were too long and were hitting my son's nerves. They were right. Another surgery to change the screws solved ninety percent of the problem! The pain subsided, and he began to get better.

This is where I got a response from God about my behavior, language, and my bad attitude toward Him.

THE DIVINE SLAP

My son needed a couple of days in the hospital to recover from the surgery, and the only recover bed they had available was in the Children's Cancer ward. First, I have to say that our doctors, nurses, and medical staff are angels sent from heaven. They are amazing people.

Like a neo-natal intensive care unit, the children's cancer ward is not my first choice of places I want to see, but I'm glad I experienced this because I learned so much. Again, it was a divine slap. I watched brave little kids and teens coping and fighting with a positive energy that I wish I could bottle up. I also saw their parents, trying to keep a brave face for their kids, but I felt their underlying pain. As I mentioned in an earlier chapter, with time, my son was going to get better. With time, their children might be gone. I was trying to fast forward time so my son would be completely better, while everyone else in that ward was trying to slow time down to a crawl. I saw amazing young people show incredible strength and resilience. They were all smiles, so why was I so pissed off? Their parents were so strong, so why was I so weak?

My son's surgery happened on Halloween of that year. One of the cancer patients was a teenage girl who made little gift bags to give to all her fellow patients. She brought my son one as well. However, it was a much younger patient that would make a lasting impression on me.

A BRIEF MEETING THAT CHANGED MY LIFE

I was in my son's recovery room. My mom was also there with us. A nurse came in and announced that the coffee cart was outside if we wanted something. Since I barely had any sleep over the previous couple of weeks, a cup of coffee sounded good.

The coffee cart had three main sections. One for coffee, one for juice and water, and one for stuffed toys. The stuffed toy section was the most popular by far. Parents and kids were buzzing around it. I went to pay for my coffee, and the attendant informed me that it was all free.

"Come on, seriously. Where do I pay?" She told me it was all covered, even the toys. "Who pays for it?" I asked. It was through Ronald McDonald Charities. How come I didn't know this? The McDonald's corporation was getting beat up in the press pretty badly at the time of this event, and yet, they kept something like this quiet. A tremendous gesture of giving to children going through hard times; something that gives children hope each day.

As I watched the bedlam around the toy cart, a little girl emerged from the crowd. She was a toddler, probably 2 to 3 years old. She was bald except for two tufts of hair along each temple. She had her own little IV stand that she pushed along with her. In her other hand, was a stuffed toy dragon. And for some reason, she made a beeline...right to me.

I will never forget her smile. It beamed.

She kept coming toward me, and her smile kept getting wider. I towered over her, so I dropped down on one knee to get closer to her level.

She stopped in front of me and raised her toy dragon up to show me, like a proud little mama. She never said a word. I commented on the dragon in a soft voice, but I don't remember what I said. She turned and scooted back to her family.

I can still see her face. I can still see the dragon. I can still see her pride and her smile. What I don't know is if she is still with us or if she has crossed over. I was divinely slapped.

After a few more days, my son was released from the hospital, and we went home. He was recovering nicely, and the pain was gone. The Stanford Medical Team solved the problem.

I was doing my best to reconcile with my Creator because I was unfair to Him. I told Him that I understood the message of the divine slap, and I thanked Him for the perspective. I continued to pray for the other kids and families that I saw in the Children's Cancer ward that week. I hope they all made it okay, but I'll never know for sure.

Then, I saw her face again in my mind. The girl with the dragon plushie. Why did she come to me? What made her have the courage to walk up to a 6 foot 3, over 200-pound stranger with that confidence, that swagger, and that joy to share it with me? It was at this time I realized that she was sent. There was a deeper meaning. A deeper request. I was supposed to do something! But what?

I didn't have to wait too long for the answer. There were thirty beds in the Children's Cancer ward at that time. It was mid-November. The message she was sending was for me to get 30 stuffed animals and bring them to the Children's Cancer ward for Christmas. That was the message. So, I did exactly that.

I showed up on December 23rd with a couple of boxes of larger stuffed animals than those from the McDonald's Charities toy cart. 30 in total. A combination of elephants, lions, dogs, bears, and tigers. I went to the front desk and dropped them off. The hospital staff tried to collect my information, but I wished them a Merry Christmas, told them I would see them again next year, and I left.

They saw me again for another five years until Covid hit and the rules changed, but Covid didn't keep me from continuing the tradition. It just made me change tactics and send the stuffed animals via online platforms instead of delivering them in person.

We don't always see the results of our actions of good. While I was never able to see the faces of the children that received them, I know that these stuffed animals made a difference to those kids and their families. Whether it gave them hope for one more day, one more hour, or one more minute, whether it gave them something to hug to endure the pain, or maybe it even gave the surviving family members of those who have passed something to hug or remember them by. I saw with my own eyes the joy that these stuffed toys brings to these kids, so I know it makes a difference. Knowing that makes me feel incredible and makes me want to do it on a larger scale. I hope that you find something similar that you can do in your community, so we can all do our little bit to make the world a better and happier place.

LOOK UP! Who in your community is an inspiration to you?

LOOK AROUND! Let's touch some lives in a positive way! Let's make some kids smile and give them hope!

LOOK AHEAD! How can we make giving and caring a daily habit?

CHAPTER 39

UNIVERSAL NET WORTH

"You cannot get through a single day without having an
impact on the world around you. What you do makes
a difference, and you have to decide what
kind of difference you want to make."

—Jane Goodall

"The unexamined life is not worth living."

—Socrates

Net worth is often used in the business world to gauge a company's success. It is a financial driver that impacts a person or business' ability to measure value. Net worth is calculated by taking the net value of assets (what is owned) minus the net value of liabilities (what is owed). But are we using the right formula to calculate the value of someone's entire net worth accurately?

My net worth to the world and to the people around me should include additional variables. Variables such as emotional intelligence, kindness, awareness, thoughtfulness, and a willingness to share the assets that measure my financial net worth to create an exponential, positive impact on the world. The value of my financial net worth improves if I keep and grow my assets and minimize my liabilities.

If there is a need in the world and good can be done by sharing assets, my act of sharing reduces my financial net worth, but dramatically increases a new measurement we should also consider.

I call it "Universal Net Worth." Universal Net Worth is calculated by recognizing the positive impact we make in the world, or in an individual's life from the sharing of our assets.

Universal Net Worth can never be accurately counted or quantified because everyone's Universal Net Worth is unique. It consists of the skills, passions, and gifts that you were given at birth, combined with how you use them for growth and share them with the world.

We can measure the impact of our Universal Net Worth by observing how it changes the life of the receiver in a specific instance: the smile you create or the tears of joy you cause. We may never know what that gesture did to change the trajectory of someone's life, or more importantly, the trajectory of their legacy.

I am reminded of a story that my Uncle Ed once told me. He was approached by a homeless person at a fast-food chain in his city. She asked for money to buy some food. He declined to give her money, but he took her inside to buy her a meal. Fast forward several years later and who does he run into in that same fast-food place? The formerly homeless woman was now in the same restaurant, well-dressed, employed, and buying her own food.

Universal Net Worth doesn't have to be measured by financial donations alone. We can offer our time and our talent to a worthy cause. We can rescue a pet. We can adopt a child and give them a loving home. We can pick up litter at the park or the beach. We can offer a kind word, a hello to a lonely person, a phone call to support a friend, or a hug. Or we can improve our self-care and mental health to have a more positive attitude and energy to put into the world. All of these are Universal assets that we can share to increase our Universal Net Worth.

Think for a minute about what little changes you can make in your life to improve your Universal Net Worth. Do I really need to watch that re-run on television again, or can I take that negative screen time to call a friend, do a workout, walk my dog, or spend positive time with my family?

"If every single person who has liked you in your lifetime, were to light up on a map, it would create the most glitteringly beautiful network you could imagine. Throw in the strangers you've been kind to, the people you've made laugh, or inspired along the way and that star-bright network of YOU would be an impressive sight to behold.

You are so much more than you think you are. You have done so much more than you realize. You're trailing a bright pathway that you don't even know about. What a thing. What a thing indeed."

— Donna Ashworth, Poet

"Love people loudly.
Tell them often.
Cheer them on as they go after their goals.
Hug them (if they like hugs) every chance you get.
No one ever got to the end of their life and thought,
'I wish I'd left more people wondering about how much I cared.'"

— Lori Deschene, Author Tiny Buddha

"If I have any lasting worth, it will be because I have tried to make people remember what the Earth is meant to look like."

— Mary Oliver

LOOK UP! You're worth more to this world than you think!

LOOK AROUND! Your real net worth to the Universe is not just measured financially. It is measured in every good thing you do to put light into the world.

LOOK AHEAD! How will you deploy your time, talent, and treasure to increase your Universal Net Worth?

KEEP GOING! Continue to increase your Universal Net Worth!

CHAPTER 40

YOU'RE TOO...

"You'll never be too much for someone
who can't get enough of you."

—Unknown

"To be beautiful means to be yourself. You don't need to be
accepted by others. You need to accept yourself."

—Thich Nhat Hanh

"You're too...fill in the blank."

Have you ever had anyone say this to you before? Have you ever heard it said to someone else? How can someone be too much of a good thing?

"You're too..."

"I'm too what?"

Too kind?

Too loving?

Too interested?

Too much?

Too nice?

Too picky?

Too sensitive?

Too critical?

Too what?

There's an old adage that "you can't have too much of a good thing," so I would argue that hearing someone tell you that "you're too" is not a bad thing if followed by a positive trait.

"You're too nice" to me is not a bad thing.

"You're too murderous" is definitely a bad thing.

While you might not like to hear "you're too," what that person is likely trying to do is set a personal boundary on how to best interact with them. So, anytime you hear "you're too" from someone, it shouldn't be taken personally, it should be taken to heart. The person saying this to you is merely establishing a level of how much of your personal gift or quality they are comfortable receiving from you. "You're too" isn't an indictment, it is constructive feedback, a call to self-examination, and an opportunity for personal improvement.

ARE YOU TOO NEEDY?

Has anyone ever told you that you were needy? You know what? I probably am! You know why? Because we only get one shot at this life, and one of our God-given rights is the "pursuit of happiness," so I'm likely going to be "needy" sometimes in that pursuit. Or, more accurately, I'm probably pursuing something that I think I WANT in my life, rather than something that I NEED. Is there something wrong with needing people in your life? Needing friendship? Needing love and affection? Needing validation from those you care about? Needing help? The answer to these questions is "no." Having needs makes you human.

There is nothing wrong with being needy if you put some healthy boundaries and expectations around those needs. You can't do everything on your own! You need other people in your life. If someone is not interested in that type of relationship with you, then go find new people who might share your vision. Life is too short to need something positive in life from someone who is not interested in pursuing happiness with you. When another person is not on the same page as you, that doesn't make you needy, and it doesn't make them a bad person. Don't take it personally when these things happen. Keep pursuing your needs and your happiness.

Self-examination is healthy. It helps us focus on how much and with whom we share these unique gifts in the future. That said, these gifts are part of the light you bring to the world, so don't ever turn off that light completely. Think in terms of deploying a dimmer switch. The light is always on in the background, but you can choose when to shine it and how brightly to shine it. You are too nice, too kind, too thoughtful, too compassionate for a reason. You are "too" whatever for a reason: for a destiny that only you can fulfill! Keep being "too!"

Remember, not everyone you interact with is meant to stay in your life forever. The give and take of each relationship will determine where they fit in your concentric circles of relationships and how much of your time and your gifts you should invest in carrying that relationship forward. To some people, you might be seen as "too much," but to others, you might be not enough, or you might be the perfect amount.

Astronomers in search of extra-terrestrial life look for planets in what they call "The Goldilocks Zone." Not too hot to support life, not too cold to support life, but "just right," similar to Earth's conditions. I maintain that this is how we should approach "You're too." Find that "Goldilocks Zone" of just right in terms of how much you share your unique gifts and who you share them with. It gets back to setting your own boundaries and respecting others' boundaries.

Let's look at the other side of the "you're too" coin. "You're too" is a personality trait, a quality, a gift given to you by God. I'm too nice? How is being nice a bad thing in a world where kindness is lacking?

God made us all "too" much of something for a specific reason. He gave us each gifts that we are supposed to share with the world, a group of people, or maybe just one person in particular. Maybe He made you "too nice" because that one friend needed a level of niceness that only you could give them in a particular time of need.

God made me "too" in different ways for reasons, so I will keep being "too" because it's who I am. I will continue to learn where and when I should adjust my behaviors and maybe be less "too" with certain individuals or in certain circumstances. I will learn how to better deploy my personal dimmer switch on that particular gift or quality, but I won't ever shut that light off because it is a part of who I am and part of the unique set of gifts I bring to the world.

Simon Sinek wrote a great book called *Start With Why: How Great Leaders Inspire Everyone to Take Action*." The book focuses on identifying your unique personal or business mission. This same principle can be applied when we ask, "What are my 'too's?'" These "too's" are the unique talents and gifts that tap into your unique heart, your unique soul, and your unique mind. How and where you share these unique "too's" is part of your Universal Net Worth.

More than ever, we need people to be more kind, more thoughtful, and more compassionate. We live in a world where corruption, evil, division, and lies are gaining ground. We must lead the world out of this darkness with our unique lights! Shine them brightly! Be "too!!!"

"You were never asking for too much,
you were just asking the wrong person."

— Bianca Sparacino,
in A Gentle Reminder

"Be yourself, no base imitator of another, but your best self.
There is something which you can do better than another.
Listen to the inward voice and bravely obey that.
Do the things at which you are great,
not what you were never made for."

— Ralph Waldo Emerson

"You will always be 'too much' for some...too loud...
too soft...too this...too that.
But you will always be perfect for the people
who really love you."

— Danielle LaPorte

TOM-ISM: "Don't take it personally. Take it to heart."

LOOK UP! If someone says, "you're too," don't take it personally. Take it to heart! Adjust your dimmer switch, but keep being ALL YOU!

LOOK AROUND! Who in your life appreciates how "TOO" you are?

LOOK AHEAD! What do you want to be "Too Much" of in the future? Get started today!

KEEP GOING! Learn to harness and share your gifts with the world in the right amount!

CHAPTER 41

IDENTITY AND DEFINITION

"Accept no one's definition of your life, define yourself."

— Robert Frost

"Everyone sees what you appear to be,
few experience what you really are."

— Niccolo Machiavelli

You often hear of people saying they "need to find themselves." This usually involves some sort of elaborate trip to go on a quest to discover who they really are. My Uncle Ed once said about these people, "Take a look at your driver's license. That'll tell you who you are!" While I find this comment humorous and somewhat accurate, it is only accurate on a surface level. Our driver's licenses show a snapshot of us in time — a photo, our height, weight, and address. Our birthdate is likely the only thing on that driver's license that will never change. And maybe your eye color, although there are procedures for that now as well. Everything else on your driver's license is variable.

When I searched "definition of identity" on Microsoft Bing, it returned the following as the top option: **"The fact of being who or what a person or thing is."**

So, how would you define yourself? What variables and characteristics would you use? What do you want people to think about when they think of you?

We live in a society that seems intent on defining who we are and placing us into some sort of identity bucket by their definition. These definitions consist of:

Ancestry

Race

Religion

Sex

Sexual preference

Height

Weight

Age

Place of birth

Where we live now

Marital status

What we do for a living

Political Party Affiliation

Attachment styles

Enneagram

Myers-Briggs

The Five Love languages

Baby Boomer

Millennial

Gen-X

Gen-Z

Extra Hot Venti Vanilla Latte With Two Pumps Delivered In The Pike Position...OK, maybe I took this a little too far.

The point is that some people and media organizations are trying to divide us into tribes to decide who or what we are based on a specific narrative, or by our appearance, rather than by really getting to know us. The list of categories I mentioned above is not complete, and people are making up new definitions and new words every day! To know who I am according to these other groups, I would need to study a new language altogether! Sorry, but I already define myself by one term alone. I am a Child of God. The rest of these definitions are man-made and interesting only as conversational topics to me.

While it may be helpful or interesting for us to learn more about these parameters, how we apply them to our lives, and how we see ourselves in light of them , the bottom line is that we are all Children of God (COGs), or children of the Universe, if you want to look at things that way. This is the foundation of how I choose to define myself. We are all uniquely created with unique characteristics, talents, interests, and gifts, so that means there are over 8 billion definitions or identities on this planet that need to be considered if we want to be accurate.

Make sure people can identify you, but never let them define you! You define who you are with your identity and how you apply and deploy your unique gifts to evolve that identity. Remember how God introduced himself to Moses? He just said, "I AM."

"Man requires three things in Life: Identity, Stimulation, and Security and the most important of these is Identity."

— David Sheldrick

"I am what I am."

— Popeye

"The most wonderful thing about Tiggers is that I'm the only one."

— A.A. Milne

There is a poem by William Ernst Henley called "Invictus." Mr. Henley ends the poem with a most profound description of "identity":

"I am the master of my fate; I am the captain of my soul."

Identity and definition. You get to decide who you are, not anyone else. Do not let others define you! Do not let others group you into a category! You are unique! You get to choose your identity. You are the Captain of your Soul.

LOOK UP! Look in the mirror! What do you see? Look inward! Who are you at your core?

LOOK AROUND! Be the definition of how you see yourself, so others will see you in a similar light.

LOOK AHEAD! Who and what do you want to become? Where are you going? What is the best way to get there?

CHAPTER 42

ALONE OR LONELY? (LONELINESS)

"Someone told me the other day that he felt bad for single people because they are lonely all the time. I told him that's not true. I'm single and I don't feel lonely. I take myself out to eat, I buy myself clothes. I have great times by myself. Once you know how to take care of yourself, company becomes an option and not a necessity."

—Keanu Reeves

"If you feel like you don't fit into the world you inherited it is because you were born to help create a new one."

—Ross Caligiuri,
Dreaming in the Shadows

I remember going to mass as a kid and into young adulthood at Queen of Apostles parish in San Jose, wanting to make sure that I attended a mass presided over by Fr. Jim Mifsud. I have had the great honor of being influenced spiritually over many years by Fr. Jim and by Fr. Brendan McGuire, who is currently Pastor at St. Simon's Parish in Los Altos, California, and whose sermons I still listen to on his podcast, *Father Brendan McGuire – Podcasts that Break open the Word of God.*

The section of the mass just after the Profession of Faith is called the Intercessions. During the Intercessions, we pray for the list of the mass intentions. These are several prayers that are offered by the church and the community. They are usually read by a lector, but at some masses, the attendees are asked to add to the list of prayers themselves. At Queen of Apostles, Fr. Jim always took the time to pray for "the lonely, the sick, and the dying." The lonely group always confused me. I get the sick and dying group, but lonely? If you're lonely, just call some friends, your family, or go do something. I didn't fully understand what lonely meant back then, but I do now. In fact, I came up with the following Tom-ism to define the hell of loneliness:

TOM-ISM: "Death is not the opposite of life. Loneliness is."

Death is the end of a life on Earth, but living a life of loneliness is not a life. People who suffer from loneliness experience a little death every day.

There is a difference between being alone and being lonely. Being alone means that you just happen to be by yourself at a given time, or you choose to take time to yourself. Being lonely is different. Loneliness is a condition where you are by yourself but don't want to be. It is a condition wherein it seems like no one else in the world sees you, hears you, or cares about you. It seems that you don't matter to anyone. Even if that isn't the case, the perception is so strong that it quickly becomes reality. Loneliness can lead to mental illness or depression, and it can be very difficult to escape once you get stuck. Loneliness is quicksand!

Loneliness is something that many people, including me, struggle with from time to time. People suffering from loneliness can be good at covering it up by putting on a happy face in public. This is why I frequently encourage and remind people to reach out to friends, family, and others who are alone on special occasions or holidays, or even every day, to let them know that you thought of them and that they matter. Sometimes, just knowing that someone cared enough to check up on them is all they need to get through the day.

If you find yourself in a loneliness spiral, take some action! Deflect and redirect your thoughts to something positive. Get out of your house! Take a walk! Walk the dog. Call a friend on the phone while you take that walk. Get yourself in a different environment. If the spiral continues, seek out professional help. Get yourself to an urgent care clinic, an emergency room, or dial 9-8-8 for the mental health hotline.

Grief can compound loneliness, whether that grief is from the loss of a relationship, a divorce, or, worse yet, a death. Community is important when dealing with this loss. Leverage your inner circles of personal relationships for companionship, support, and reassurance.

Loneliness can lead to desperation. Desperation can lead to bad decisions like addiction, substance abuse, spending money on retail therapy, or clinging on to a relationship, however bad, to have some sort of human interaction.

The best thing you can do in life, whether you are lonely or not, is to get to know yourself. Look inward. Count your blessings. Make a list of the things that you like best about yourself. Make a list of the things that bring you happiness and joy, what I have called Trees of Joy. Make a list of the things that bring you hope for the future. What vision do you have for your life? These are the things I call Anchors of Hope. Take positive action towards those things. Invest in you! Become the best version of you that you can be.

If you hear yourself asking questions or making statements like:

- → Why am I always alone?
- → Why doesn't anybody like me?
- → Why won't anyone listen to me?
- → I can't do that.
- → I wish I had her life.
- → I don't belong here.
- → God, I'm okay if you just take me now.

It's time to seek some professional help to correct that thinking. You do belong here. You have gifts to share with the world that the world needs. You may never see or know the results of sharing your gifts, but trust me, by sharing them, you are touching lives in a positive way.

Loneliness is a feeling of not belonging. It is born out of a perceived lack of purpose. Once you identify your why (or multiple 'whys') you can turn your loneliness to action. And with that action will come some level of interaction, whether positive or negative, with others. Once you make the decision to no longer wallow in your loneliness but to act on your purpose, you will change the world or create a world where you feel a stronger belonging, even if you take the action all on your own!

Is our loneliness a reality or something we talk ourselves into? Is our loneliness tied to unrealistic expectations? Is our loneliness triggered because we can't have what we want when we want it or by a lack of timely response from the person we reached out to? What makes you feel lonely? It is important to understand that feeling and what leads to that feeling to be able to deal with it in a healthy way.

A Bloomberg article in August of 2022 said, "'sad' is the most searched word by teenage Gen Z listeners on Spotify."

According to a recent study published by the Indiana University School of Medicine's Institute of Aging:

- → 40 percent of British adults go without a daily conversation.
- → 60 percent of people aged 18 – 24 are "lonely."
- → Loneliness is worse for health than obesity, alcohol, or smoking 15 cigarettes a day.

So, based on these statistics, loneliness is a real problem in society. How many of these people have experienced suicidal ideation? How many of you reading this have experienced that at some point in your lifetime?

As I shared earlier, loneliness is something I've struggled with in my life over the years, and it's something that still comes up from time to time. I've learned to identify it when it starts to come along, and I've learned where I contribute to it. Maybe I feel it because I'm a private person. Maybe too private. Maybe too selective. I don't like crowds, but I'll go to Disneyland, I'll go to sporting events, and sometimes I go to these places alone! I was joking with my daughter the other day and told her, "I try to get out and meet new people, but it's always too crowded."

If you start to feel lonely, it is important to deflect that feeling immediately before you start to sink in the emotional quicksand. It is always important to remind yourself that YOU MATTER! We all matter! We matter more to other people than we think or know. People are busy. People have many priorities in life, especially if they have kids. The fact that they are busy doesn't mean that you're not important to them.

How should someone deal with loneliness? Each person will be unique in how they cope. I would strongly suggest that you consult a counselor or therapist for tips on how to deal with your unique situation and feelings. I am not a professional therapist or a medical doctor, but for me, I deal with it in various ways.

First, if you are looking to plan something and want to invite someone along, it is important to have the perspective that you are extending an invitation, and it is not an obligation on the other party. If I ask someone to join me in doing something, it is because I enjoy their company, I want to get to know them better, or I know that this activity is something that they might enjoy. That said, if they decline, I don't let it stop me from going, even if I go alone. Life is too short to miss out on doing things that are important to you!

Some say if you can eat a meal in a restaurant by yourself or go to a movie by yourself, it demonstrates mental strength. I've spent many nights eating alone while on business trips. Sometimes these business trips were to foreign countries. My colleagues in Europe were always kind enough to invite me to dinner, but I knew they had wives and families, so I would either grab a quick pint with them or meet them in the morning for coffee or breakfast instead, which was more convenient for them and would not take them away from their families. You learn to deal with eating alone.

Second, when you're feeling lonely, find something of interest, and go do it! Turn on a TV show you like. Watch a movie that you find entertaining, whether it makes you laugh, smile, or inspires you. You can also take a walk or a hike in nature. You can go to a sporting event, art gallery, museum, or concert. Turn your loneliness into dedicated "me time" instead, but I recommend that you change your environment when you feel it coming along! Make sure to get out and do something that enriches you in some way, rather than staying home or in your hotel room staring at the walls or a screen.

Thirdly, think about it! How many times have people invited you to attend things that you've turned down? Sometimes, we contribute to our own loneliness by not saying "yes" when we could have. If you say "no" on a regular basis, you might be building your own wall with that person. Try to say "yes" more and show up!

There are a lot of great comments and quotes focused on loneliness and being alone. I want to start with a couple of examples, one from Steve Jobs (who I met once!) and the other from Ruby Dhal, a British-Afghan poet.

STEVE JOBS

"In other eyes, my life is the essence of success, but aside from my work, I have little joy. And in the end, wealth is just a fact of life to which I am accustomed. At this moment, lying on the bed, sick and remembering all my life, I realize that all my recognition and wealth that I have is meaningless in the face of imminent death. You can hire someone to drive a car for you, make money for you – but you cannot rent someone to carry the disease for you. One can find material things, but there is one thing that cannot be found when it is lost – "LIFE." Treat yourself well and cherish others.

"…If the house we live in is 300 square meters, or 3,000 square meters – the loneliness is the same. Your true inner happiness does not come from the material things of this world. Whether you're flying first class, or economy class – if the plane crashes, you crash with it. So, I hope you understand that when you have friends, family or someone to talk to – this is true happiness."

— Steve Jobs

That last line from Steve Jobs about having friends really strikes home. We don't need a lot of friends or family, just some strong relationships that we can rely on when we need companionship. On the other side of the loneliness coin is quality alone time. The time that we need to spend with ourselves or maybe in discussion with our Creator. Ruby Dhal challenges us to "be brave enough alone."

"Be brave enough to be alone.

And by alone, I mean not depending on someone else for your happiness, I mean dreaming of a future where your goals rely on you, and only you, to achieve them.

By alone, I mean strolling down a beach with the sand between your feet and hugging yourself as the wind brushes against your arms,

I mean taking yourself on a date to your favourite café with a book and a coffee and watching the sun rise and fall back down again, feeling nothing but comfort in that moment.

Be brave enough to love yourself...

Be brave enough to be there for yourself...

Be brave enough to become the right person for yourself, because if you're brave enough to do what's right for your heart, then I promise you – you will never feel lonely when you're alone."

— Ruby Dhal

President Theodore Roosevelt offers the following, diving a little deeper into the subject of quality alone time: "The farther one gets into the wilderness, the greater is the attraction of its lonely freedom."

This is the dual-edged sword of being alone versus loneliness. If I take a walk deep into a forest because I enjoy nature, that is the "lonely freedom" that President Roosevelt mentions, but I'm not lonely. I'm enjoying the experience. And maybe even enough to invite someone to come with me next time!

When you are in a state of loneliness, you will often doubt yourself or question your abilities or accomplishments. It is important to remember that you have talents and unique gifts to share with the world. Share them!

We are often our own worst critics. This self-criticism can often lead to that loneliness spiral into quicksand. I need to get better at remembering what I tell others and apply my advice to my own life. We also need to remind others how great they are and how we see them, because they don't see themselves through our eyes. As the Persian poet Hafez once said, "I wish I could show you when you are lonely or in darkness, the astonishing light of your own being."

"When you reach the end of your rope, tie a knot and hang on!"

— Franklin D. Roosevelt

I will take the opportunity to throw in a Tom-ism, given FDR's quote about hanging on to a knot in a rope. Sometimes people are at the end of their rope and have run out of knots if they feel lonely.

TOM-ISM: "You never know when you might be the last knot on someone's rope."

"I used to think the worst thing in life was to end up all alone. It's not. The worst thing in life is to end up with people that make you feel alone."

— Robin Williams

I love Robin Williams. He made me laugh a lot. He made others laugh a lot. But he was hurting deep inside, and no one knew. No one suspected. There were (are) times where I feel like maybe I have a little or a lot of what Robin Williams had. This is why I keep saying that it is important to reach out to people and let them know that they matter, particularly around the tougher days for lonely people: the holidays, birthdays, and maybe anniversaries of the deaths of their loved ones. We are all fighting internal battles, and we all need reminders of the fact that we matter in this world.

"Sometimes God puts you in places alone, because He needs you to realize you do NOT need anybody but HIM!"

— Unknown

If you have faith, then this quote is self-explanatory. When you are feeling lonely, maybe it's time to **LOOK UP** and talk to your Creator.

We've all been in situations where we feel like we don't belong. When you sense that feeling coming on, it is time to take positive action. Act like you belong in the room because you do! Find a friendly face and start a conversation. Order a drink from the bar and talk with the bartender. If neither of these opportunities present themselves, you can always move on to a different place altogether and see if that room is more comfortable. Finally, if you don't fit in at a place, maybe it's because you're supposed to be building a new place!

There is an important distinction between being alone and being lonely. Being alone is a strength. It can help us better understand ourselves. It can help us build a stronger relationship with our Creator. It can help us examine our hopes, our dreams, our needs, and our boundaries. Make sure you carve out some quality, healthy, alone time.

LOOK UP! Pray for the lonely, the sick, and the dying.

LOOK AROUND! Who in your concentric circles of relationships might need you to throw them a rope to help pull them out of their quicksand? Let them know that they matter.

LOOK AHEAD! Who do you want on the journey with you? Invite them to join you! Say "yes" to them if they invite you!

KEEP GOING! No matter what! You are here for a reason **NEVER GIVE UP!**

CHAPTER 43

GPS

"Go forth in every direction – for the happiness, the harmony, the welfare of the many. Offer your heart, the seeds of understanding, like a lamp overturned and re-lit, illuminating the darkness."

—Guatama Buddha

"I am realistic – I expect miracles."

—Dr. Wayne W. Dyer

The initials GPS stand for "Global Positioning System." GPS leverages a network of satellites in space. It is used by airlines, shipping companies, trucking companies, and the military for navigational purposes. GPS systems are now built into our cars and mobile phone applications to let us know exactly where we are, to give us directions to places we've never been before, or to provide us with the best route to our desired destination.

I have a different meaning for "GPS" when I want true direction in my life. Like the network of satellites, I look to the heavens for my version of GPS, where the "G" stands for God, and GPS stands for:

God Provides Salvation

God Provides Security

God Provides Sustenance

I can also provide a different definition for GPS in terms of how I can make the world around me a better place. All these new definitions of GPS focus on positive action that improve my life and the world around me, rather than some moniker like "Getting Pretty Stoned." These new, positive ways to define GPS include:

God's Productive Servant

Get People Started

Go Plant Seeds

Give People Something

Greatness = Purpose + Success (or you can substitute "standards.")

Give, Provide, Share

"When you get what you want, that's God's direction. When you don't get what you want, that's God's protection."
— Shannon L. Alder

"Never underestimate the power you have to take your life in a new direction."
— Germany Kent

It's a personal choice, but I encourage you to build a close relationship with your God and Creator. Many people do this through religious communities, prayer groups, Bible studies, or some other formal means. While these things can be very rewarding, you don't need to go to a church or an official building to have a relationship with God. Just talk to Him! Start talking to Him today. Talk to Him at the beach, on a hike, at the mall, on the freeway, in your office, in your classroom, or wherever else you might feel the need. Earth is His church!

Everyone's relationship with God is unique. My relationship with Him is personal, for me to pursue and understand alone. That doesn't mean I shouldn't share my faith with others to help them pursue their own unique relationship with God. Maybe I can plant a mustard seed...

TOM-ISM: "If you do God's work, He will help you do yours."

LOOK UP! Which of these definitions of GPS help define your life?

LOOK AROUND! If you're lost, check your GPS. If others ask you for directions, point them to their GPS.

LOOK AHEAD! How can you use these definitions of GPS to give your life a new direction?

CHAPTER 44

A.I.=ANGELIC INTERVENTION

"If there is anything that links the human to the divine, it is the courage to stand by a principle when everybody else rejects it."

— Abraham Lincoln

PRAYER ADVOCATES

Prayer is energy.

Thoughts and prayers do mean something. At a minimum, thoughts and prayers put focused, positive energy into the Universe on someone's behalf. This doesn't always mean that you will get the desired result; God has a say. Still, we can lift people up by letting them know that we took the time to send a request to the Almighty on their behalf. How do you feel when someone tells you that they prayed for you, or that they will pray for you, or that they will continue to keep you in their prayers? To me, it feels nice that someone cares enough to think about me and to advocate to the Heavens on my behalf. It is positive energy, and positive energy is sometimes enough to nudge someone in the right direction or even change a life entirely.

THE MORE IMPORTANT A.I.

The emergence of Artificial Intelligence, or A.I., is something that people, businesses, and governments are trying to sort out. What will be the impact on jobs? How will A.I. help us to become more efficient? What if A.I. is used by someone with evil intent?

The future of A.I. and its overall impact, whether net positive or net negative, is yet to be known. So, I will learn as much as I can about it to know how to live with it, make a living on it, or live around it.

Regardless of what the impact of A.I. will be, I know that I always have and always will manage my life around my own definition of A.I. You see, well before the topic of Artificial Intelligence made its way into the global landscape, there were centuries of stories of a different kind of A.I., the kind of A.I. that I will choose to rely on, regardless of the net effect Artificial Intelligence will have on the world. This is the kind of A.I. we will need to harness to take care of each other as new challenges present themselves.

What is the A.I. that I will rely on? My A.I. stands for Angelic Intervention, and for my purposes, I will equate Angelic Intervention with Divine Intervention. I believe in an afterlife and that our souls go to a different place after death . What is that place? Is it still here on Earth, but in a different dimension, or is it somewhere in the heavens as depicted by most religions? If I believe in an afterlife for our souls, it makes sense to me that the souls of my ancestors, angels if you will, would do whatever is allowed by divine law to intervene on my behalf, should I ask for their help. And before you make the argument that God is all-powerful, so all you need to do is ask Him, I agree with you, but maybe God delegates. Maybe God says to my grandfather (Pop) in heaven, "Send an elephant named 'Lemaiyan (Blessing)' over to Tom's Jeep in the middle of nowhere in Kenya." Maybe God says to my grandmother in heaven, "Fly that monarch butterfly past Tom's face while he's thinking about what next step to take in his life." Maybe God says to my dad, "Yes, go ahead and have Tom's Lyft ride stop in traffic behind a car that has your initials on its license plate while he's struggling with a career decision and saying, 'Dad, I wish you were here to talk about this.'" (For anyone interested in investigating this topic further, read the book *Signs, The Secret Language of the Universe* by Laura Lynne Jackson.)

We ultimately make our own decisions and choices and live with the consequences of those decisions. However, I believe those little voices in our heads, those flashing lights we sometimes see, animals that cross our paths, number sequences we often encounter, and a whole other host of unexplained phenomena are manipulated energy from some other dimension or place. There is a world of angelic and divine happenings out there that we may or may not perceive and don't fully understand. There's angelic intervention happening around us all the time, but especially when we ask or pray for something. It doesn't mean that we will get the specific outcome we request, but it does mean that we have advocates in another realm that at least listen. It also means that however lonely we may feel in the physical realm, we are never truly alone in the spiritual realm.

Yes, that Artificial Intelligence A.I. may ultimately destroy us... but Angelic Intervention A.I. will lead us to our salvation.

TOM-ISM: "Don't let man-made institutions get in the way of your relationship with God."

LOOK UP! Angels are watching over us!

LOOK AROUND! Who needs your thoughts and prayers?

LOOK AHEAD! Artificial Intelligence will have an impact on your life. Learn how to navigate it!

KEEP GOING: Angelic Intervention is always available to us if we ask for it!

CHAPTER 45

FAITH

"To one who has faith, no explanation is necessary.
To one without faith, no explanation is possible."

—Thomas Aquinas

"Faith is taking the first step even when
you don't see the whole staircase."

—Dr. Martin Luther King, Jr.

Faith is very personal and unique to each of us as individuals, even if we choose to express our faith in a particular religious community. Faith is a one-to-one relationship with your Creator based on what you believe. While your faith can be shaped by man-made or church-made influences, the core of your faith is your personal relationship with God.

There have been times in my life where I have said, "I wish just one part of my life would go right." I've had friends tell me the same thing about their lives. We tend to get bogged down by these types of thoughts when it seems like things are not going our way, but I finally realized that there is something I can always get right, regardless of what else is going on in the world, and that is a strong relationship with God. God is the one thing that always goes right.

My faith is not the same as your faith, and it is not my job to convert you to my faith but to share my faith with you in ways that are anchored in love, respect, and understanding. Faith is belief without concrete evidence. That said, there is always plenty of circumstantial evidence to support our faith. There are different levels of faith:

- → Faith in your God
- → Faith in yourself
- → Faith in others

All require a level of trust built over time. All require a strong level of belief. I've recently taken leaps of faith to help support my kids' dreams, so why would I hold back on my own? "A ship in harbor is safe, but that's not what ships are built for" is a great quote from John A. Shedd. What good is a ship if it never goes anywhere? It can't explore, it can't deliver goods, and it can't carry passengers, so it just takes up space. Don't just take up space! Weigh the anchors! Leave the harbor! Get tossed on the high seas, but get out of the harbor, off your couch, and go do what you were built for!

Let me be clear: I am advocating for responsible leaps of faith. This doesn't mean that you sell your house or take all the money out of your kid's college funds and go buy a motorcycle to travel around the country. It means listening to that little voice, that divine nudge, that tells you to pursue your purpose and share your unique gifts.

"Faith is not belief without proof, but trust without reservation."

— D. Elton Trueblood, Quaker theologian and chaplain

"Faith is unseen but felt.
Faith is strength when we feel we have none.
Faith is hope when all seems lost."
— Chatherine Pulsifer

"Worry is a down payment on a problem you may never have."
— Joyce Meyer

"Remember that God will answer your prayers in His own timing and in ways you might not expect."
— Tony Dungy

DON'T WAIT! TAKE A LEAP OF FAITH!

As I write this, I have about twenty-five percent of my life left to go by the averages. What have I done with it? Well, quite a lot, but not nearly enough. Why do I say this? Because I have many ideas and talents that I haven't shared. Why haven't I shared them? Probably out of fear. But what am I afraid of? Failure, criticism, mediocrity, maybe even actual success?

I found a series of quotes that I believe most accurately reflect our faith journey. In the Bible, Matthew 17:20 states that faith can move mountains. So, if we have faith and start praying for things based on that faith, another quote from an Craig Greenfield applies: "I've found that if I pray for God to move a mountain, I must be prepared to wake up next to a shovel." If I question why I must have enough faith to move a mountain, and why this mountain is in my path, I can also cite another mountain reference by Mel Robbins who said, "You have been assigned this mountain to show others that it can be moved."

Faith does not mean that we ask for something and expect it to be done without our involvement. We have a responsibility to work toward our goals and purpose. As Bishop Thomas Dexter Jakes says, "Faith is the substance of whatever it is that we hope for. The important thing is that we teach that faith is connected to good works and responsibility." We don't get to sit on the couch and wait for others to deliver what we hope for, we must do the work as well.

Take a step forward now! Today! Overcome the fear. If something is in your path, take a step sideways or slightly backward until enough light illuminates the next logical step forward. You must be brave enough to be bad at something new until you learn and grow with each new attempt and each new lesson. The world needs you to share your gifts! The world is waiting for you to stop being its best kept secret. Put it out there! Measure the reaction. Take the next logical step. Keep improving. Most importantly, touch lives. You'll never fully know the impact you have had on the earth while you're on it, but maybe someday, you'll be able to see it from somewhere else.

TOM-ISM: "F.A.I.T.H. = Following Angelic Instructions To Heaven."

LOOK UP! Face your fears!

LOOK AROUND! Who are the people in your life that you know you can always go to in a time of crisis?

LOOK AHEAD! What is your purpose? What are your goals in life? As Theodore Roosevelt said, "Believe you can and you're halfway there."

KEEP GOING! Your faith will be rewarded!

CHAPTER 46

FORGIVENESS

"The simple truth is, we all make mistakes,
and we all need forgiveness."

—Desmond Tutu

"It is one of the greatest gifts you can give yourself, to forgive."

—Maya Angelou

I think the most famous quote regarding forgiveness is from Alexander Pope, "To err is human, to forgive, divine." Some people think that forgiveness is for the weak, but forgiveness takes courage, and it is a sign of maturity and strength. Mahatmi Gandhi agrees: "Forgiveness is an attribute of the strong."

I would argue that if you truly want closure on a bad situation, you must be forgiving. You need to forgive yourself first and foremost and learn how to forgive others who may have wronged you. Forgiveness is a magic word. Forgiveness is the password that opens the door to personal peace, happiness, and freedom. While holding grudges or seeking revenge is a natural human reaction to being wronged, it is also a personal prison. The only way to escape this prison is to forgive.

Truly forgiving someone, including yourself, is easier said than done. When we are wronged, our initial reaction is not to turn the other cheek. We want accountability at a minimum and possibly restitution or maybe even revenge on those who wronged us.

I am human, like everyone else, and there are sins I don't think I could ever forgive. As I've mentioned before, I don't believe Hell is a real place or a destination, but for those who would murder, rape, torture, kidnap, or commit crimes against children or animals, I would help construct such a place. Does this make me a forgiveness hypocrite? Maybe.

I try my best to forgive those who wrong me, but I don't forget. I don't forget because their actions changed our relationship and changed our dynamic of trust. You can still forgive someone and still not completely trust them again. You might even decide to dismiss them from your life for good or at least create distance and not give them as much access to you as they had before. The level of forgiveness we grant is up to each of us individually, but remember that forgiveness is a gift we give to ourselves, not the person we are forgiving.

"Forgiveness is a strange thing. It can sometimes be easier to forgive our enemies than our friends. It can be hardest of all to forgive people we love. Like all of life's important coping skills, the ability to forgive and the capacity to let go of resentments most likely take root very early in our lives."

— Fred Rogers

I mentioned Father Jim Mifsud earlier. Father Jim was our parish priest, pastor, and family friend. Mostly, he was my dad's friend, but we all loved him. He was a priest of the people. He liked to get his hands dirty. He got involved in the community and put his faith into positive action. I was lucky to have him as a spiritual advisor in my youth and young adulthood. Father Jim once said that "the people closest to us will hurt us the most." I think this is mostly true. We do not expect the people closest to us to hurt us. But Father Jim is right: the people closest to us are the ones we are most invested in emotionally. This makes the people closest to us either the easiest to forgive, because we want to get back to a normal, loving relationship with them, or they can be the hardest to forgive because the pain runs deeper.

"To forgive is to set a prisoner free and
discover that prisoner was you."

— Lewis B. Smedes,
Author and theologian

Forgiving someone who wronged you is one of the toughest things to do, but it is also the most important because forgiveness sets us free, not them. They are still accountable for having wronged us, but if we continue to hold a grudge, resentment, or a desire for revenge, we are impeding our ability to pursue our passions and purpose. We are spending energy on something that pulls us down rather than propels us forward. Easier said than done.

"Forgiveness is a favor we do for ourselves,
not a favor we do to the other party."

— Rabbi Harold S. Kushner,
When Bad Things Happen To Good People

When you do not forgive, you stay in the quicksand, and the longer you wallow in being unforgiving, the deeper you sink. You can forgive someone for wrongdoing, but you don't have to forget, and you don't have to relieve them of the accountability of their actions. What you are doing is reframing your mind to prioritize what is in your best interest, rather than wasting time and energy thinking about how you were wronged.

Fool me once, shame on you. Fool me twice, shame on me. Fool me again and again, I'm the idiot. Yes, you can be too forgiving. As Maya Angelou once said, "When someone shows you who they are, believe them." This is sound advice. I wish I had heard and applied it earlier in my life. Don't be fooled by the same person multiple times. Forgive them, but don't forget. And be more vigilant if you choose to keep them in your life.

To move forward into the light of a brighter future, it is important to cast off the chains of past pains that hold our attention and distract us from moving forward. Forgiveness is a key part of casting off that pain and drawing clear boundaries to avoid being hurt like that again. Author Paul Lewis Boese says, "Forgiveness does not change the past, but it does enlarge the future." I agree that we can best enlarge our futures by becoming more forgiving of others, but mostly by making sure that we first become more forgiving of ourselves. Forgiveness is more than a magic word and more than a password. Forgiveness is the rope that gets us out of the quicksand and puts us on solid ground toward a better and brighter future.

TOM-ISMS: "Forgiveness is essential, but some sins are so great only God can forgive them."

"My Lord and Savior doesn't want anyone killed for 'blasphemy.' He forgives and tries to change hearts and minds. Worst thing that I heard Him do was lose his temper, yell, and flip over some tables."

LOOK UP! Forgive yourself first!

LOOK AROUND! Who can you forgive to help free yourself?

LOOK AHEAD! Try to be more forgiving as you move through life.

KEEP FORGIVING, so you can **KEEP GOING!**

KEEP GOING... WE'LL GET THERE!

CHAPTER 47

STONE SOUP & BUILDING COMMUNITY

"Children see magic because they look for it."

—Christopher Moore

"Be happy for no reason, like a child. If you are happy for a reason, you're in trouble because that reason can be taken from you."

—Deepak Chopra

When I was growing up, there was a popular morning children's show called *Captain Kangaroo*, starring Bob Keeshan. *Captain Kangaroo* was a popular TV show for kids before *Sesame Street*. And yes, it was productive screen time for me! Other characters on the show included Mr. Green Jeans, Bunny Rabbit, who would always find a way to steal Captain Kangaroo's carrots no matter how well he hid them, and Mr. Moose, who was always pranking the Captain. The show would start the first of every month with a birthday cake for all the children in the audience that were celebrating a birthday that month.

Another feature of the show was that Captain Kangaroo would read books to his TV audience. One the books that stuck with me the most was *Stone Soup* by Marcia Brown, originally published in 1947. *Stone Soup* is a tale of three soldiers returning home from war who come to a village. They are tired and hungry, but the villagers see them coming, hide all their food, and deny them any lodging in their homes. The three soldiers declare they are hungry and they will make stone soup. The villagers have never heard about stone soup and are curious to know what it is. The soldiers ask the villagers to bring out a large pot to fill with water and three stones. The villagers agree to help. The soldiers then begin to list ingredients to make the stone soup taste better, if they only had them. And the villagers begin to produce these ingredients from the hiding places in their homes. Ultimately, a delicious soup is made that feeds all the soldiers and the villagers, and a good time is had by all. The soldiers are invited into some of the villagers' homes to spend the night before they continue their journey the next morning.

The moral that I take from the story is this:

TOM-ISM: "If everyone gives what they can, even if it is a little, collectively, it can benefit an entire community."

Stone Soup reminds me of a story my dad told me about his mother and father during the Great Depression. He said that his mother would make large pots of soup and share it with the community. Every house would contribute something or take turns feeding the hungry in their neighborhood by sharing whatever they could afford to give.

LOOK UP! What positive things are missing from your community that you can contribute?

LOOK AROUND! Who in your community needs some assistance?

LOOK AHEAD! What flavor of Stone Soup will you make?

CHAPTER 48

KEEP GOING!

"Listen to your gut. The pull. Don't be afraid. If you can't stop thinking about it, then you want it, have wanted it, and will continue to want it. Dive straight In and ride it out. The wave will carry you. Simply trust the water."

—Victoria Erickson

"We can't allow ourselves to be frightened into not living our lives... We have to keep going with the faith that things will get better... And things will get better when we make them better."

—Oprah Winfrey

In an episode of the *Gotta Look Up* podcast, I spoke about an experience I had where I witnessed people going through various forms of hell. We all find ourselves in some form of personal hell from time to time. The key is how we react to and deal with the personal hell when it shows up in our lives.

"Keep going" is advice I tend to give to anyone who is going through a difficult time. The only way out is through, so you need to keep going. I use this advice quite a bit but tie it to a quote from Winston Churchill: **"If you're going through hell, keep going."**

I have a small, pewter paperweight on my bureau in my bedroom with Churchill's quote inscribed. I bought it during my divorce when things were at the height of insanity and darkness.

It makes sense. Keep going! Don't stop. Don't loiter. Don't slow down. Keep moving forward and put hell behind you. Once I share this quote with people, I only need to say, "Keep going," and they understand the context.

So here I am, the guy who keeps telling people to get off their phones, sitting in church when a flood of creativity comes into my brain. At my age, these ideas don't always decide to settle in and nest; they just keep going. In one ear and out the other, as my mom would say.

So, I pulled out my phone to write down my "church notes." If the priest ever catches me, I can always show him my "church notes," so he knows that I was paying attention and not doom scrolling during the homily. So, let's look at my church notes, because the topic that ran wild in my mind was about Hell.

I don't believe in Hell, at least not the way that most religions describe it. I believe that Hell exists, but I don't believe that Hell is a place or a destination that we go to in the afterlife. If I believe in an omnipotent, omnipresent, all-forgiving God, then a permanent hell cannot exist because He would forgive everyone's sins before allowing them into heaven. Here is a bonus Tom-ism for you: **"Hell is distance from God."**

"Somebody once told me the definition of hell: On your last day on earth, the person you became will meet the person you could have become."
— Anonymous

So, if Hell is not a physical place or destination, then what is it? To me, Hell is a set of conditions or circumstances that test us on Earth. Hell is in our minds, and everyone's hell is unique. Hell is mental quicksand that can take form in any of the following:

- → Expectations
- → Regrets
- → Lost loves
- → Grief
- → Financial struggle
- → Pain
- → Hunger
- → Loneliness
- → Depression
- → Unfulfilled potential
- → Illness
- → Divorce
- → Societal pressures
- → Other man-made things

How do we get out of Hell? First, we need to recognize what hell we are in and take some action to get out of that hell. Once we take that initial action, then we keep going. We find our Trees of Joy and our Anchors of Hope to get out of hell and quicksand. Take action! Keep going!

Hell is minimized by LOVE.

Hell is minimized when we shine our LIGHT into the DARKNESS.

Hell is minimized by any of the following:

- → Love
- → Light
- → Joy
- → Caring

- → Truth
- → True justice
- → Hope
- → Alignment
- → Passion
- → Purpose
- → Abundance
- → Nature
- → God-made things

"No matter where you're at in life, it only takes one big win to set you up forever. KEEP GOING!"

— Unknown

"One must go on working silently, trusting the result to the future."

— Vincent Van Gogh

LOOK UP! Keep Going!

LOOK AROUND! And Keep Going!

LOOK AHEAD! And Keep Going!

KEEP GOING! No matter what! Never Give Up!

CHAPTER 49

BLAZE A TRAIL AND LEAVE BREADCRUMBS

"If you could only sense how important you are to the lives of those you meet, how important you can be to the people you may never even dream of. There is something of yourself that you leave at every meeting with another person."

—Fred Rogers

"One day you will tell your story of how you overcame what you're going through now and it will become part of someone else's survival guide."

—Johbag Mnola

In the tale of "Hansel and Gretel," the two children ventured deep into a forest and left breadcrumbs so they could find their way back home. Prior to GPS systems in our cars and phones, we used physical maps and found landmarks on the road to help find our way back or learn how to get somewhere in the future.

As we move forward on these new trails we are blazing, it is important for those of us who have been down the path to take note of the journey and leave instructions to those who will follow. Be a guide to help them navigate the same or a similar path. This may take some effort or, as with the case of the UXB Bomb Diffusers in London during World War II, it may take some sacrifice. During the London Blitz, many German bombs remained unexploded and needed to be diffused so as not to create more death and destruction. This life and death work was conducted by the Royal Engineers and is depicted in a television show entitled *Danger UXB*. There are records written by the bomb diffusers that list the step-by-step procedures they used to take apart the bomb to render it harmless. Such entries include something along the lines of "cutting the blue wire now," which ended up being that engineer's last entry. The next Royal Engineer to come across the same ordinance would then know not to cut the blue wire to diffuse that type of bomb.

Although the UXB example is an extreme case of leaving breadcrumbs, it shows the importance of sharing our knowledge downstream to help teach those who follow how to better navigate the path, so they can apply that knowledge and improve upon it. We owe it to future generations to share our knowledge, leave maps and blueprints, give advice, and offer direction.

From these experiences, we learn and evolve. We can help others go through their own journeys by sharing what we've seen, so they can experience the same things through their own unique perspective and can better understand how to navigate their way through. This is how pathways are carved out to become dirt trails, then dirt roads, then paved roads, and finally highways.

Every day we are given an opportunity to blaze new trails and expand our horizons. We can learn new things, have new experiences, meet new people, and achieve personal growth. Are you taking advantage of all the potential new experiences in front of you, or are you looking backward, thinking the best years of your life have passed? Are you stuck in the present, not knowing where to go next? Take a step in a different direction. Explore new interests, read new books, travel to new places, and try new hobbies. Learn! Every day is a new opportunity to learn new things that either serve us or are not of interest to us. Either way, it is another step toward understanding our passions and purposes. Blaze that trail and help others who might want to follow by sharing your experiences.

TOM-ISM: "Believe that you will always find a way! Ask others for directions!"

LOOK UP! Where can you blaze new paths?

LOOK AROUND! What new experiences do you want to have? What new things do you want to learn?

LOOK AHEAD! Where will you go next? When you go, make sure to leave a trail of knowledge for others to follow.

KEEP GOING! Your purpose is looking forward to meeting you!

CHAPTER 50

DEATH

"Live as if you were to die tomorrow.
Learn as if you will live forever."

—Mahatma Gandhi

"People living deeply have no fear of death."

—Anais Nin

Somebody died today. They took with them the love, the pain, the knowledge, the struggles, the talents, and the victories of their daily life.

They left behind loved ones and family members who are now grieving. They took with them a wealth of knowledge and a bridge to not only their family's past but our collective past.

They took with them the realities and history of the times they lived through. They took with them knowledge of the world's greatness, faults, love, hate, priorities, and culture, whether right or wrong, that spanned their lifetime. They took with them a perspective that could guide our current times and culture if we are willing to listen and learn rather than judge.

There is an African proverb that says, "When an old man dies, an entire library burns down." When someone dies, they take with them all of their accumulated knowledge, wisdom, and instincts. If they failed to write things down or pass their knowledge on to the next generation, all that they have discovered, learned, and known is buried with them.

You see, everyone lives through happy times and difficult times, and everyone lives through these times via the lens of their perspective, their biases, the biases of others towards them, and the influence of other people, experiences, and other cultures. It is important that we hear their stories, store their knowledge, and take advantage of their wisdom.

We don't have all the answers today just like we didn't have all the answers yesterday, last month, or ten years ago. We do our best, at least I hope we do, to improve our lives and the lives of others. We can never get anything to be perfect, but we can always strive to be better. We must give each other grace in that process.

We can only be better if we are willing to have an open mind, listen to others, and try to meet them on equal terms as Children of God, not as members of a political party, a religion, or a particular tribe.

The Stoics have a saying: "Momento Mori," which means "Remember, death is inevitable." We all know the adage "The only thing certain is death and taxes."

There are some things worth dying for. In The Bible, John 15:13 says, "Greater love hath no man than this, that a man lay down his life for his friends." What are the things that are worth dying for to you? For me, the list is as follows:

- → My God
- → My kids
- → My family
- → My freedom
- → My country

I would probably also add a scenario of finding a cure for a fatal disease. God forbid you are ever put in this position, but let's say you're inflicted with something and the only option that you have available to extend your life is to take an experimental drug or have an experimental procedure done to you. Wouldn't you take that chance? Wouldn't you want to know that the test on you may have saved other's lives?

Many in the military would say that they would give their life for the person in the fox hole next to them…and many have.

My faith tells me that death is the end of a physical life and marks the beginning of an afterlife that I cannot comprehend but that is "paradise." My faith tells me that death allows our souls to cross over into this next life. It gives me hope, and hope matters.

CEMETERIES

I have visited cemeteries where family members are buried, where historical figures are buried, and ones that are tied to famous battlefields like the American cemetery in Normandy, France. I have visited the site of the D-Day landings. If you ever get the chance to get to Normandy, I encourage you to go. Go to see the rows upon rows of crosses and headstones at the top of a cliff overlooking the English Channel. Go to see the distance these brave soldiers had to travel to get off the beach and up the hill. How exposed they were to the German armaments on top of the cliff. How far they had to run and how hellish it must have been.

Regardless of the cemetery I visit, I pay my respects and reflect on the contributions made by the people buried there and how they impacted my life, whether directly, in the case of family members and friends, or indirectly, in the case of historical figures or fallen soldiers. I focus on the numbers in the birthdates and the death dates to see if there are any numerical patterns or dates that tie into other things. I focus on the dash in between the dates, finding it ironic that an entire lifetime is represented by a simple dash (-).

FUNERALS AND MEMORIALS

I also find it interesting that we wait until someone is deceased to discuss how much they meant to us. I saw the following quote from an unknown source: "Everything we say at funerals should be said at birthdays instead." I wholeheartedly agree! We may embarrass the heck out of the person, but they should know the positive things we think about them while they are still with us. We should repeat these same things when they cross over as well, but then it will be an encore performance of things we have already said.

Whenever I attend a funeral or a memorial service, I try to talk about the best qualities of the person who has crossed over. I'll talk about my fondest memories and funniest moments with that person. I try to get people to laugh, and I try to get them to cry because that is how we honor those who are important to us: with laughter, tears, and hopefully tears of laughter.

But I also believe that death does not end us. I believe that our souls move on to a better place. I also believe that those who have crossed over may still be trying to communicate with us by sending us signs from the other side. I still talk to people that have crossed over. I still ask them for guidance and direction in difficult times. In her book, *Signs, The Secret Language of the Universe*, Laura Lynne Jackson discusses ways that those who have crossed over can send us signs through coins, feathers, number sequences, and by animals that cross our paths. I be-lieve Lemaiyan was one such sign for me, but I hadn't read the book then! Since reading the book, I have seen many different signs; so have other members of my family. I don't always understand what the sign is trying to convey, but it offers a level of comfort and a reminder that even when I am by myself, I am not alone, and others are looking out for me. In his book, *Tuesdays with Morrie*, Mitch Albom states, "Death ends a life, not a relationship." Paulo Coelho adds to this notion of continuing a relationship with our loved ones after they die with this quote: "We never lose our loved ones. They accompany us, they don't disappear from our lives. We are merely in different rooms."

Yes, somebody died today. They started their day not knowing of their fate. They had plans, expectations, joy, and fears. They took all of that with them, but they couldn't take any of their material assets, money, real estate, or any physical gifts that you gave them. It is common knowledge that you can't take those things with you. But I believe there is something you can take with you to the other side, and that something is the love we plant in other's hearts during their lifetimes. They can take with them how we made them feel and how we loved them. That love is energy they can take with them to the heavens. That is why it is so important to show people how important they are to us in this life and let them know how much we love them.

Somebody was also born today, and there are family members who are ecstatically happy at their arrival. What love, knowledge, talents, and victories will be experienced by them to maximize their lives and happiness and minimize their pain and struggles? This new life brings new hope! What will they do to improve our world? What good things will everyone say about them? Let's agree to teach all newborns around the world, regardless of race, creed, or culture, to LOVE, not to hate...and let's see what happens!

"Some people die at 25 and aren't buried until 75."
— Benjamin Franklin

"Death takes the body.
God takes the soul.
Our mind holds the memories.
Our hearts keep the love.
Our faith lets us know we will meet again."

— Kelly's Treehouse

LASTS

There is an adage "nothing can last forever." The Stoics said, "Memento Mori." A day will come for each of us that will be our last, but life is full of "lasts."

The last time you hold your daughter's hand.

The last time you pick up your son and carry him.

The last time you went to school.

The last time you played on a playground.

The last time you hit a baseball.

The last time you danced.

The last time you took a special trip.

The last time you smiled at a stranger.

The last time you watched a sunset.

The last time you put your toes in the ocean.

The last time you pet your dog.

The last time you hugged a loved one.

Make sure to make everyone of your "lasts" create a lasting memory!!!

TOM-ISM: "After we have a moment of silence to honor the dead, we should continue to honor them with moments of laughter, smiles, conversations, and tears to honor all they mean to us."

LOOK UP! Live a little!

LOOK AROUND! Who are the most important people in your life that you need to spend more time with? Tell them how important they are to you!

LOOK AHEAD! Life is short! How can we maximize the time we have left?

KEEP GOING! Add more length and depth to that dash!

CHAPTER 51

LIVE IT UP!

"The key to immortality is first living a life worth remembering."

—Bruce Lee

"Tell me, what is it you plan to do with your
one wild and precious life?"

—Mary Oliver (poet)

Life. You only get one. As Franz Kafka once said, "The meaning of life is that it stops." We need to remember this, as each day is a new beginning in our lives, but that day could also be our last. We need to LIVE life to the fullest every day!

As I write this, most actuarial tables would give me about twenty more years to live. I am in my early sixties (or, as I like to say, my "sexties," and I'm hoping this Tom-ism catches on!) So, given this reality, I have lived about seventy-five percent of my life, and I have another twenty-five percent to go. Does that scare me? No. It inspires me to make sure I do the things and travel to the remaining places on my list. It inspires me to love more and focus more on the people who are important to me. It gives me a new focus.

Many of us take life for granted. Many of us think we have unlimited time. Many of us wait for perfect conditions before starting on a path. Life doesn't work that way. There's no better time to pursue our passions than right now! Don't wait for perfection!

Don't say, "When X happens, then I'll do Y." Start now! I recently saw a social media post that said, "Someday is not a day of the week." Actually, it is. Someday is every day of the week. Turn your "someday" into today to start living the life you were meant to live. There's a life inside you striving to get out. One of the people I follow and admire is Trent Shelton, and I think he said it best: "You're a choice away from a new beginning and a commitment away from a new life." Decide the life you really want and go live it!

You were given life at this time for a reason. To use your unique gifts for a specific purpose. To learn, to teach, to love, and be loved. To make friends. To explore. To be the best version of yourself. None of us were created to live our lives staring at screens. We were created to do the things that excite us, that make our hearts beat faster, that challenge our minds and bodies, that give us a sense of pride and accomplishment when we're finished. I don't know about you, but I don't get this kind of rush from behind a desk working for someone else, even though I am grateful for the blessing of an income to fund my needs and wants.

"Life shrinks or expands in proportion to one's courage."
— Anais Nin

"It is not length of life, but depth of life."
— Ralph Waldo Emerson

Do you remember that feeling of the school year coming to an end and summer vacation about to begin? That childhood perception of freedom! Time to focus on adventure and play. We need to get that feeling back as adults. We need to do it in a responsible way, as the burdens and bills tied to adulthood fall on us now rather than our parents, but we need to get that summer vacation vibe back in our lives.

Life is about creating memories. We create memories that span generations. If we're lucky, we have memories of great-grand-parents, and if we're even luckier, we will create memories as a great-grandparent. But regardless of how long our lives are, we are here to create memories for ourselves, for those we care about, and even for people we may never see again who re-member us from a brief encounter in a flashing moment of time. These memories can be simple, a shared sunset, a hug, a great conversation, an accomplishment, the day we met a loved one, the day our kids were born, the day we got the promotion and the raise, the day we quit our jobs to pursue our passions, our first snow, putting our feet in the ocean, looking for shapes in the clouds, and countless other things that are deeply personal.

"Be a curator of your life. Slowly cut things out until you're left only with what you love, with what's necessary, with what makes you happy."

– Leo Babauta, Writer

ANY REGRETS?
Never regret a day in your life.
Good days give happiness,
Bad days give experience,
Worst days give lessons,
And best days give memories.

– Unknown

We hear people say all the time, "I have no regrets." Yes, you do. We all do. We all look back on our lives and wonder what might have happened had we taken a different path. What would our lives have looked like? We'll never know, so it is healthiest to process regret as a learning experience for the future. The benefit we have is that we can learn from the regrets of others, particularly those who have lived longer than we have. We also have the obligation to share our regrets with those who follow us in life, so they can use our learnings as they navigate their future. I found the following list of *The Top Five Regrets of Dying* by Bronnie Ware:

5 Regrets of Dying by Bronnie Ware:

1. I wish I'd had the courage to live a life.

2. I wish I hadn't worked so hard.

3. I wish I'd had the courage to express my feelings.

4. I wish I had stayed in touch with my friends.

5. I wish I had let myself be happier.

I find the last one to be the most profound because happiness involves many variables and choices. Many of those choices encompass the other four items on this regret list. So have the courage to live the life you want. Find that ideal work-life balance and work hard enough to be able to live the life you want. Have the courage to express your feelings, and don't worry about the reaction of others, instead, be proud that you made your intentions and desires known. Make it a priority to stay in touch with your friends! Let yourself be happier! Start making changes today to minimize regret.

"Don't fear failure so much that you refuse to try new things.
The saddest summary of a life contains three descriptions:
could have, might have, and should have."

— Louis E. Boone, Author

"For whatever it's worth, it's never too late to
be whoever you want to be...
I hope you live a life you're proud of,
and if you find that you're not,
I hope you have the strength to start over."

— F. Scott Fitzgerald

"When I stand before God at the end of my life, I would hope
that I would not have a single bit of talent left and could say,
'I used everything you gave me.'"

— Erma Bombeck

If I look back with an open mind and an open heart, I have lived a wonderful life with wonderful experiences and memories. But I'm not done! There's more life to live and more experiences and memories to create. I am laser focused on this as I come into the backstretch of life, but unlike a jockey going to the whip to finish the race faster, I am taking my sweet time and making my time sweeter. (That actually makes a great Tom-ism! "I'm taking my sweet time and making my time sweeter.")

LOOK UP! What life have you led so far? Are you happy? If not, what needs to change?

LOOK AROUND! Who is important in your life? Tell them often. Keep them close as you go forward.

LOOK AHEAD! Do you have any dreams yet to be fulfilled? Get going! Don't wait for perfection! Take some action and continue to build along the way.

KEEP GOING! Live it up! Be a light! Leave it all on the field! Share all your gifts with the world before your time is up!

CHAPTER 52

LOVE ONE ANOTHER

As I mentioned at the beginning of the book, I love to collect quotes that I find profound. So, I am going to include a plethora of quotes on Love in this final chapter.

I already covered the topic of love in previous chapters, but love is probably the most important variable in our lives. Love brings us into the world, and, hopefully, love continues to be part of our lived experience all the way to the end. Many people don't feel loved. How can we change their lives by showing them just a little bit? Love builds faith in oneself. Faith builds our confidence, and confidence helps us pursue our purpose. Love!

"Where there is love, there is life."

—Mahatma Gandhi

"Love is what counts, because a person comes into this world with nothing but love and leaves it again with nothing but love."

—Unknown

"Where there is no love, put out love and you will draw out love."

—St. John of the Cross

"Our Lord does not look at the greatness of our actions, or even at their difficulty, as at the love with which we do them."

—St. Therese of Lisieux

"People grow when they are loved well. If you want to help others heal, love them without an agenda."

—Mike McHargue

"If there is any immortality to be had in us human beings, it is certainly only to be found in the love we leave behind."

—Leo Buscaglia

"Love is the only force capable of transforming an enemy into a friend."

—Dr. Martin Luther King, Jr.

"And if, when it is all over, I am asked, what I did with my life – I want to be able to say – 'I offered love.'"

—Terri St. Cloud

"Spread love everywhere you go. Let no one ever come to you without leaving happier."

—Mother Teresa

"A new command I give you: Love one another. As I have loved you, so you must love one another." This is the commandment that Jesus left to the world according to John 13:34 in the New International Version of the Holy Bible. We can never love each other as perfectly as He loves us, but we can try. We can certainly do better than we are doing now. "Love one another" seems pretty simple, yet we make it more difficult. We make it difficult because we get lost in the pursuit of more instead of the pursuit of happiness; lost in competition instead of cooperation; lost in trying to be right instead of trying to be loving.

We will never get this "love one another" thing completely right, but we should pause, reset, and at least make the attempt. I often hear people say, "What can one person do?" Well, if all 8 billion of us think that way, then nothing will happen. Here's what we can do. We can lead by example. We can do a better job of being loving each day. Imagine if all 8 billion of us did that!

"Love One Another!"

LOOK UP! Try to be Loving instead of trying to be Right.

LOOK AROUND! Who in your life needs more of your Love?

LOOK AHEAD! How much better will your future be with more Love in it?

KEEP GOING! Keep Loving more and more!

WHERE I CAME FROM & WHERE I'M GOING

I remember having a conversation with my son about life and alignment. He was going through a period of frustration in moving forward on a career path. I told him that it was normal, but that he could not fast forward; he could only move at a pace controlled by him and the universe, and that when he was trying to move faster than the universe, he was not in control and needed to be patient. He needed to take the next step each day and peek inside each door put in front of him. Some doors he will walk into. Some doors he will close. Some doors he will need to knock down. What finally resonated with him was when I said, "When a man is not aligned with his purpose, he first gets frustrated, then maybe gets a little angry, but then ultimately he gets depressed." My son was quiet for a bit and then replied, "When did you become a philosopher?" I told him that I've just lived longer and observed my life and other lives longer than he has.

This alignment with purpose is an important point to what changed for me in recent years. We all have dreams and visions. We all have God-given gifts that we don't always get to open, use, and share with the world. Why? Sometimes out of fear; sometimes out of doubt or imposter syndrome. Many of us struggle with this. I know that I did and still do. But self-doubt and fear are forms of quicksand. I've gone through many jobs in recent years, and each has led to a dead-end within six months to a year. Why? Because I was not in alignment with my gifts, my purpose, my Creator, or the Universe. I was focused on the small, the safe, and the comfortable.

With each job loss and self-examination of what to do next, the conversation with God went something like this: "I don't get it. What do you want me to do?" This was met with the divine reply: "I've given you gifts you don't use, and I want you to use them." But I would once again find myself being pursued by recruiters for yet another new career opportunity that would keep me comfortable and pay the bills. I would take it and end up in the same predicament. So, this last go-round, I said, "OK, God. Here we go! It's you and me. I'm taking the leap." I started *Gotta Look Up*, created some content, started a podcast, wrote a book, and I found some great teammates to help me launch it and move it forward.

Little did I know that when I launched the *Gotta Look Up* project in October 2023 with a focused message, mission, and movement of Love, Forgiveness, and Peace, during that month, the doors of hate and war would open on a global scale. Maybe it was divine timing. Maybe my unique voice needs to be heard, but will anybody listen? Will anybody take messages of Love, Forgiveness, and Peace to heart in a world that seems hellbent on hate, division, and conquest? Will my messages be amplified? My faith tells me that most people will find courage if they see others showing courage and speaking out for truth, love, and what is right, so keep going. Keep talking. Keep living in purpose. Keep trying to do the right things.

To continue moving forward on my journey, I am going to continue working to improve my skills, learn new things, travel, deepen my faith, and try to be more caring, kind, and understanding in all my personal interactions. I am going to do my best to create memories with people that will touch their hearts, their souls, and hopefully create a legacy of good and joy, even if my name is not attached to it.

To that end, I challenge you to STOP doing the following:

Stop being your own worst critic.

Stop waiting!

Stop holding on to things.

Stop holding on to relationships that do not improve your life.

Stop wasting time!

Stop the negative self-talk.

Stop all disbelief!

I'm sure there are other things that you would add to this STOP list that are personal to you. It is important to recognize these things, address them, and turn them into positive actions.

I also challenge you to START doing the following:

Let's all be positive COGs! (COG = Child of God, or at least be a Citizen of Good if you don't believe...yet.)

Let's turn fear to action.

Let's turn racism to "Gracism." We can eliminate racism by treating all people with grace and respect.

Let's be hopeful and helpful.

Let's forgive and let go but not forget.

Let's get out of the quicksand through Trees of Joy and Anchors of Hope.

Let's turn hate into LOVE!

Let's be the strong hands that hold other hands.

Let's be the strong shoulders that help carry others' burdens.

Let's be thoughtful minds that remember to show people that they matter.

Let's be the strong hearts that love our neighbors.

Let's be the shining light in darkness!

Let's LIVE with passion and purpose rather than just exist!

Let's have faith in ourselves and our Creator to live the lives of our dreams!

The final Tom-ism to close out this book and **LOOK AHEAD** with more conviction is yet another thing that I want you to stop, and it leads to taking positive action in the direction of fulfilling your purpose. This affirmation is what motivated me to launch *Gotta Look Up* and try to make a positive difference in the world:

TOM-ISM: "Stop being the world's best kept secret."

What does this mean? It means that we have all been created for a purpose. We've all been given gifts unique to us that will help each of us fulfill that unique purpose. Take action! Take a small step each day toward fulfilling that purpose. Open the gifts that your Creator gave you and have the courage and faith to share them! The world needs them! You won't always see the end results of sharing your gifts, but they do make a difference. Don't leave them unopened!

I have spent most of my professional career chasing the next job, the next raise, and the next promotion. I've seen other people engaged in the same effort, wanting to build their little organizational empire. I was living the wrong life. I was not aligned with my purpose. I was not sharing my gifts. I was focused on man-made definitions of what success meant. That is, until I came to this realization:

295

"I don't need my own empire. I'm helping Jesus build a kingdom." (another Tom-ism!)

ACKNOWLEDGEMENTS

It is said that writing a book requires at least two people. One to write it, and one to tell you when to stop writing. In my case, no one told me to stop writing, but many people inspired me and helped me along the way. All glory and praise to my God, and my Lord and Savior, Jesus Christ who helped me write this book. Many times, I found that the words and ideas would just show up in my mind as I was typing away. Coincidence? Maybe coincidence is nothing more than a timely miracle. (**Tom-ism**?)

First, to my family. You have always been there to support me in good times and bad. You are familiar with many of the stories in this book and many other moments of light, and some of dark, in my life. I love you all immensely!

Second, to my friends. Some of you are also familiar with the stories in this book. Your help, words of encouragement, and taste of my own medicine in telling me to "keep going" are greatly appreciated. I love you all as well!

Third, to Brandon Janous, Jodi Cowles, Rachael Mitchell, and the tremendous team at Blue Hat Publishing for your advice and creativity in walking me through this process, holding my hand at times, and making me accountable. I met Brandon at one of Bob Goff's Writers' Workshops that I attended at The Oaks near San Diego. So, I also must acknowledge Bob Goff, Kimberly Stuart, and Taylor Hughes, who led the workshop, for their great instruction and advice in getting stories out of my head and on to paper. I also need to thank my fellow class-mates in that particular workshop. A great group of creative people who help each other and encourage each other and share experiences of their author path so that others can learn from those breadcrumbs.

Finally, to my father. The man who raised me and encouraged me to pursue this passion, to study greatness, and to always do my best to make a positive difference in the world. I miss you every day and hope you are proud of this book!

And to you, the reader. Thank you for staying with me all the way to the end! I hope you found some enjoyment, encouragement, and inspiration to change your life in a positive way.

ABOUT THE AUTHOR

Tom Campbell is a child of God; one of five children; and a father of two. His passions include animals, history, nature, sports, travel, and writing. Tom has a goal of visiting all 50 U.S. states and as many countries as he can get to. Tom is a follower of Jesus Christ and believes that actions are the loudest prayers, and that God can be found everywhere, not just in a church, so constantly seek Him!

Follow Tom on Instagram: @tom_campbell24